E N D

From the Land of the Rising S⌐ ... ⌐ moving story of a young, displaced Japanese girl who seeks to find her real self in the often confusing culture of America. As Junko fights for her own self-esteem, she discovers— or is discovered by—a God who loves her, accepts her, and has a unique plan for her life. In a day when millions of young people seek to be the next American Idol, or the latest Christian imitation, Junko's example encourages us to find our identity in God and in serving him. People of all ages will enjoy this delightful story, filled with humor, joy, and humble wisdom. But From the Land of the Rising Sun will be especially powerful for young women and men who are desperately trying to be somebody, to be accepted, and to find their way in a complex and crazy-making world.

—Mark D. Roberts, senior director
and scholar-in-residence for Laity Lodge

Having lived in Japan when I was a young, I can relate well to Junko Cheng's testimony of feeling displaced in a foreign country. From the Land of the Rising Sun is a well-woven tapestry that blends God's faithful love with his divine plan, that if received, will lead us to a future and a hope!

—Wayne Cordeiro, senior pastor
at New Hope Christian Fellowship, Honolulu, Hawaii

I am so grateful that Junko has written out her story of faith! Hearing how the Lord has worked in others' lives gives us the opportunity to see the life lessons that He wants to teach us—and one of the lessons I'm sure you'll see in Junko's life is the truth of our trust in God. His children never need to run in fear from Him: He is a Father that we can run to in trust.

—Tom Holladay, teaching pastor
at Saddleback Church in Lake Forest, California

Junko first crossed my path in 1993 during our inaugural "Spotlight" competition for independent Artists at the Gospel Music Association in Nashville. For nearly twenty years since, she has warmed the hearts of audiences on many continents the same way she first warmed ours that day in Nashville. How wonderful that her written words in this book can speak to individuals everywhere the way her music has. Bringing these chapters into your life will grow your appreciation for her music. I hope that you are as fortunate as I have been to encounter both.

—FRANK BREEDEN, founding chairman of the Academy of Gospel Music Arts / GMA, former president of the Gospel Music Association (1997–2003), managing partner of Premiere Authors Literary

Junko's story is everyone's story. We may not be able to carry a note, but we all have a song within us that is waiting to burst forth…a song about a misplaced childhood, a forgotten culture, a hidden hope, or a dangled dream. Junko's story is a message of encouragement, especially to those who have their heritage in another land.

For years, Junko has blessed my children, my grandchildren, and my church family with her music and her presence. Her story has revealed to me why she is such the blessing. God is good. He took a scared little girl from the Land of the Rising Sun and transformed her from her idea of "not so special" to God's idea of "very special."

—CORY ISHIDA, senior pastor,
Evergreen Baptist Church of San Gabriel Valley

From the Land of the Rising Sun

OF THE

Rising Sun

A Journey to Acceptance, Identity & Belonging

JUNKO NISHIGUCHI CHENG

FROM THE LAND OF THE RISING SUN
published by Junko Nishiguchi Cheng
© 2011 by Junko Cheng

International Standard Book Number: 978-0-615-48776-2

Cover design by Kirk DouPonce (www.dogeareddesign.com)
Cover photo by Kate Noelle Akamine (www.katenoelle.com)
Consulting editing by Lisa Guest
Substantive editing by Steffany Woolsey
Interior design and typeset by Katherine Lloyd (www.TheDESKonline.com)
Interior proofreading by Eileen Hall

Printed in the United States of America

For information:
www.junko.com

11 12 13 14 15—10 9 8 7 6 5 4 3 2 1

DEDICATION

To Harry and Keiko Nishiguchi,
for beginning my story.

To David, Joshua, and Megumi,
for entering into my story.

And to Jesus, the author and perfecter of our faith,
for completing my story.

TABLE OF CONTENTS

ACKNOWLEDGMENTS

*M*y heartfelt thanks go out to the behind-the-scenes team of literary professionals who made this book a reality: Lisa Guest, who edited the first pass and set me sail; Steffany Woolsey, who continued the editing process and journeyed with me the rest of the way; and to the team who waited at the dock as I sailed home—Kirk DouPonce with his beautiful cover artwork, Katherine Lloyd with her typesetting expertise, and Eileen Hall with her eagle-eyed proofreading skills.

God blessed me with so many wonderful people in my youth, only some of whom I've mentioned by name in the book. Any attempt at making a list would surely be incomplete, but nonetheless I would like to give a special shout-out to Jayme Fryer Wood and her parents, Judy Tarbell and her parents, Carol Antablin Miles, Dave and Kristin Moe Lyle, Gary and Carol Richmond, Steve Yamaguchi, Rev. George Munzing, Dave and Debbie Hansen, Mike and Lesley VanDordrecht, Kevin Kummer, Ted Limpic, and Stan White, for revealing Christ to me each in your own unique way.

I am also thankful for my friends, pastors, teachers, and small groups at Irvine Presbyterian Church and Saddleback Church for continuing to nurture me and challenging me to grow, particularly Ben Patterson, Mark Roberts, Scott Bullock, Tim Avazian, Rick Warren, Tom Holladay, Buddy Owens, and Debbie Kerner Rettino.

Many thanks to my husband, David, for persevering through this book-writing process with me, concurrent with yet another CD recording project. I am forever grateful for the love and support you continue to offer as I pursue my calling in life. You are my safe harbor.

Thank you, Josh and Meg, for inspiring me to write this book. May we enjoy many more ice cream socials together.

Soli Deo Gloria.

"The storm caught me by surprise."

It was a sunny Southern California afternoon, and the elderly patient was talking to his family physician. His statement came out of the blue, unrelated to anything they had spoken of prior to that moment. Unrelated, in fact, to the actual weather outside. "I forgot my umbrella, Doc," he continued.

He was suffering from the early stages of dementia.

EVER SINCE MY HUSBAND, DAVID, told me about the encounter he had one day with this patient at his medical office, I have wanted to use this gentleman's statement as the opening line of my very first book.

Opening lines are important, although few are as memorable as "It was the best of times, it was the worst of times" and "Call me Ishmael." I wanted an opening sentence that would capture the essence of my book, and I found this one perfect.

The storm caught me by surprise.

Okay, so we haven't exactly started the first chapter yet, so technically it's not the opening line. And I don't have dementia...yet. But hear me out.

Isn't it amazing how often we are surprised by the unexpected storms in our lives?

Relationships go bad.

We run out of money.

We get sick.

Our kids get sick.

We move.

We move to a foreign country.

We win a competition.

We lose.

And there are many, many more.

Intellectually, we know that life is all about going from one crisis to another. Storms are going to come—they're inevitable. Jesus even said it: "In this world you will have trouble. But take heart! I have overcome the world" (John 16:33).

Nonetheless, we are still surprised when bad things happen, and we're often caught without our umbrellas. Why? I suppose it's because we think that every day should be sunny and that everything should work out the way we think it ought to. We have life all mapped out, and when things don't go as planned, we are surprised, shocked, and dismayed. As if we have any control over our lives in the first place....

This book is about my life and the storms I have experienced so far, such as moving from Japan to the United States as a young girl and having to make all new friends. Learning to speak a new language. Attempting to make it in the music business. Trying desperately to catch a flight home from Brazil.

Did the storms surprise me? Why, yes! And it was not a pretty sight as I kicked and screamed my way through the many disappointments that came my way. But when the storms passed and I got a chance to assess the full situation, I was often pleasantly surprised.

God taught me a new lesson.

I grew as a result.

It made me stronger and more secure.

God never let me go.

It could have been much worse.

It turned out better than what I hoped for.

I am actually grateful for the storm!

I'm usually limited to about three minutes during my concerts to give my testimony before I launch into my signature song, "Land of the Rising Sun." I often get asked about the "rest of the story," but I never have quite enough time to do so. It would take us hours, and we'd go through lots of coffee!

So, here is my opportunity to share with you the extended version of my testimony. I'm so delighted that you picked up this book, because you are about to meet the main character of my story.

No, it's not me.

It's someone I used to be afraid of but now love with all my heart, soul, and mind.

It's someone I sometimes refer to as Mr. Thunder. Or, in Japanese, *gorogoro-san*.

Yeah, you're going to have to read more to find out.

So what are we waiting for? Let's go!

ODD GIRL OUT

For you created my inmost being;
you knit me together in my mother's womb.
I praise you because I am fearfully and wonderfully made;
your works are wonderful, I know that full well.

PSALM 139:13–14

When I was young, I was tall. Relatively tall, that is, and embarrassingly taller than my friends. My two sisters and I inherited some abnormal gene that made us sprout up and mature physically ahead of all our peers, and it looks like I've passed that gene on to my own daughter. Dear Megumi is often told that she is "so tall for an Asian"!

I always stood near the back of the line in school, and people generally assumed I was two grades older than I actually was. (How I loved being thought of as "older" back then!)

Hoping to be less conspicuous, I tried to slouch my way through the first few years of grade school. That didn't work in Japan, where I lived until I was eight and a half, nor did it work in Riverdale, New York, where I began my new life as a third grader at P.S. 24. Had I stayed in Japan, I probably would have been considered average in height—just as I am here in the States—because the current generation of young people in Japan is getting taller and taller, probably due to a more Western diet.

And speaking of diet, I had no clue as a child that we are what we eat. I thought some people were naturally thin—or not—just as I was naturally tall, and that food consumption had little effect on your predestined girth.

That lack of understanding, plus bountiful cooking by my mother, who grew up hungry in famine-plagued, post–WWII Japan and therefore made sure that her daughters never felt deprived, added up to a very big girl. I used to stand and try in vain to see my feet, but they were definitely hidden by a protruding belly filled with my mother's yummy cooking. My weight peaked when I was twelve, at which time I decided to turn from my nutritionally sinful ways.

What I took for granted then was that being big and tall has its advantages. For example, in sixth grade, I protected my friends during a melee at a Donny Osmond concert by bracing myself against a wall so they could work their way to the nearest exit. (No, they never refunded our tickets to this abbreviated concert, our first pre-teen outing.)

Also, since I could reach higher than others, I was in demand for TPing during sleepovers. I was also a faster runner and higher jumper than my friends, and teachers entrusted me with more responsibilities because my height made me seem mature and therefore more trustworthy. But such positives did not outweigh the negatives of being so large compared to everyone else.

Then—suddenly—I became small.

I didn't shrink; everyone else just started to grow. The same gene that made me sprout young made me stop growing when I reached middle school. I have grown only half an inch since sixth grade: I am almost five foot three. I say "almost" because I'm actually five feet and two and three-quarter inches tall, but that takes too much space on my driver's license. I hope it doesn't constitute a lie. But I digress.

When I entered middle school, I found myself dwarfed by all these girls who used to be scrawny, tiny, and short. They became Amazon women almost overnight! In a year and a half I went from thinking of myself as the Big Girl to the Petite One.

It took years for my brain to catch up with my new identity, and in some ways, it still hasn't.

BEFORE WE MOVED TO NEW YORK, I lived in a suburb of Osaka, Japan, in a small town called Fujiidera. Osaka is the epicenter of a certain Japanese dialect called *Kansai-ben*. It's not a true dialect in that it isn't completely foreign to people from other parts of Japan, but it does have a certain twang that I think is very laidback and friendly. Kind of like people talk in the Southern U.S.

Many stand-up comedians on Japanese television are from the Kansai area, and they use Kansai-ben liberally in their routines. This delights viewers from Tokyo and its surrounding areas, who speak their very proper dialect.

My mom used to tell me that I had a knack for catching on to accents and imitating dialects. She would laugh when I imitated a comedy duo on TV, complete with the right Kansai-ben inflections.

All that was funny until we moved to New York, where I met other Japanese girls whose families had also come to the U.S. for overseas assignment. Most of these assignments lasted for about three years, so new Japanese kids were always arriving and others leaving.

It was a pretty tight-knit community. Old-timers were expected to help out new Japanese arrivals with classroom work and translation. Every single Japanese student at P.S. 24 also attended the one local Japanese school that met all day on Saturdays, which meant we were together six days a week. These students were my first friends in my new country.

But back to the language thing. Just about every Japanese person living in New York at the time was from Kanto, which is Tokyo and its surrounding metropolitan area. They spoke the beautifully refined, high-society *Hyojun-go*, the "standard" Japanese.

I, however, was a country bumpkin from Osaka. When I arrived at P.S. 24 and opened my mouth to speak, the Japanese girls encircled me and started to laugh in delight. Until then, they had only heard Kansai-ben via comedians on TV.

I'm sure they were all genuinely entertained to hear me talk, and maybe they even secretly wished they sounded like me. But I was mortified. As a third grader in a new country, trying to fit in with the only group of people who might accept me, I was determined not to be the odd girl out. Even though I didn't speak a word of English, my first order of business was to learn standard, TV journalist–dialect Japanese.

Except for this group of Japanese expatriates, Riverdale was populated mostly with people of European descent. I had never seen real white people before. My sisters had some dolls with blond hair, but here I was standing next to an actual person with golden locks. How I wished I had beautiful blond hair.

But then I realized how ridiculous my black eyebrows would look with blond hair. I decided to leave the blond hair on white people and instead wish that I were Caucasian. The porcelain-white skin of these Americans fascinated me. My skin was dark from spending

4

every day flying my kite through the rice fields back home. I vowed right then to stay out of the sun. You see, I tan so easily that a late-fall swim in the setting sun gives me a tan that lasts through Easter.

In Japanese culture, dark skin indicates common manual labor, while pale skin suggests an aristocratic lifestyle. I could not understand why these beautiful people with their blindingly white skin rubbed baby oil on their bodies and spent hours at the pool. Especially when most of them just turned beet red!

THE SUMMER AFTER WE ARRIVED IN New York, my parents sent my sisters and me to a summertime YWCA camp in the Catskill Mountains so we could learn English. It was a weeklong camp with horseback riding, swimming, and singing. It was a whole lot of fun.

The following summer, we went for two consecutive weeks. I sang a few Japanese folk songs a cappella in the talent contest and came in third place, winning a watermelon for my cabin. I was a hero that night. In the next day's Camp Olympics, however, I didn't do as well in the holding-your-breath-underwater competition. I was nervous! My heart beat so fast that I couldn't hold my breath for much longer than ten seconds, tops. I disappointed the entire cabin that day.

No matter. The canteen beckoned with my daily snack purchase: Cracker Jack. I'd dig deep to pull out my prize whistle or sticker, and then munch on the caramel popcorn while I sat on the lawn watching a giant-screen movie about a dog that was very shaggy.

During that second visit to the camp in the Catskills, we stayed over the weekend, which meant that on Sunday morning the leaders went around gathering girls who attended church. I watched with a mix of curiosity and a little envy. I could tell there was something special about where they were going, and I wished I could be part of it.

To my way of thinking, church seemed distinctly American. No one I knew in Japan went to church. Almost everyone was affiliated with the local Buddhist temple. We went there occasionally to pray, usually asking for a specific blessing—to pass the high-school entry exam, win the lottery, for driving safety, for a healthy baby to be born. We burned incense, clapped three times, and bowed down in prayer. Sometimes we'd use a special bamboo ladle to quench our thirst with holy water; other times we'd throw coins into the slotted box out front for good luck. These things were a part of our culture, and we did them without question.

I never bothered inquiring who we were praying to, but I do remember asking Mother one time if there is a God. She said, "Of course!"

In hindsight, I realize that I probably would have gotten the same answer from just about anybody in Japan. Most Japanese believe there is a God...or a few. There are little statues of gods on the sides of the roads wherever you go in Japan, even in the major metropolitan areas. The statues wear cute little bibs and someone is always leaving a fresh fruit offering. Sometimes, on my walk home from school, I wished I could swipe an orange slice to quench my thirst. But I refrained; that would be disrespectful.

AFTER ABOUT THREE YEARS OF LIVING in New York, my family moved again, this time to Southern California. My sisters and I suddenly found ourselves the only Asians who weren't native English speakers. At that time, the few Asians who lived in Orange County were third- or fourth-generation Chinese or Japanese, and they had all successfully assimilated into the American culture. In other words, they only *looked* Asian; they were actually Asian Americans. They spoke English, no Japanese—and to my horror, they wore shoes inside their homes! In Japan, we left our dirty shoes outside.

My new fifth-grade classmates were amazed and amused to meet an actual, real-life foreigner. They couldn't stop asking me how to say this and that in Japanese. They wanted to know if I really owned a kimono (yes) and if I wore it at home (no, only for Halloween).

Most kids knew very little about my culture. This was well before anime, video games, Pokémon, California roll, and many other fine Japanese artifacts had found their way onto American soil. They would try out what little Japanese they thought they knew: *nee-how*, which is "hello" in Chinese. They would bow to me with their hands together, fingers pointing upward, as they had seen in either *The King and I* or a travel commercial for Singapore Airlines.

I quickly realized that my classmates' curiosity was an easy way to get attention, and I did the best I could to communicate with my broken English and make friends. Then one day on the monkey bars after school, one of my new California schoolmates asked me what time it was.

I looked at my watch and replied in my best Bronx accent, "It's a quarta afta foah." And they laughed at me!

My talent for picking up inflections and accents had gotten the better of me. The English I had so diligently learned in New York was not the same dialect that people spoke in California. Once again my first order of business became working on my language skills— but this time, ditching the New York accent and learning to speak like a proper Californian. I was not going to be humiliated again!

2

RICE FIELDS
AND MR. THUNDER

Out of the brightness of his presence clouds advanced,
with hailstones and bolts of lightning. The LORD thundered
from heaven; the voice of the Most High resounded.

PSALM 18:12–13

Summers are hot and humid, almost tropical, in Japan. As the temperature rises, so does the humidity.

Misery levels peak during *tsuyu,* Japan's rainy season. Tsuyu begins mid-June and lasts at least a month, sometimes longer. As if prompted by the Japanese weather service's official declaration of the beginning of the tsuyu season, clouds move into formation and begin dumping rain throughout Japan, mocking schoolchildren who are just beginning their summer break.

Because of the high humidity, nothing ever dries. Not your umbrella, not your rain boots, and certainly not your laundry, which you try in vain to dry on the clothesline that you temporarily move indoors to avoid the rain. You might as well leave the laundry outside, though, because the end result will be the same: wet clothes, even days later.

The damp clothes hanging indoors make the occupants inside already-crowded Japanese houses lethargic and cranky. The ever-churning fan can't even seem to stir the thick, hot air or reduce the growing odor of mold now permeating the walls.

We had no air conditioning back then, but one day my sisters and I got ingenious. First we stacked ice cubes in a rice bowl and placed it in front of the blowing fan. Then we put our faces up to the fan, sucked in the chilled air, and sang, "Ahhhh..." in chorus as the turning blades distorted our voices.

After about a month, Japan's weather service officially declares the end of the tsuyu season. Again, as if on cue, the clouds part to reveal the sizzling summer sun. (As a child, I was convinced that if the weather service just declared tsuyu over a little earlier, the sun could come out—and summer would begin—that much sooner.)

With the tsuyu behind us, it was time to take everything outside to let dry. This included the children, who by now had perfected origami, the folded-paper art that I am convinced was invented by Japanese parents desperate to keep kids occupied during tsuyu seasons.

Only the droning cicadas drowned out the sounds of kids laughing and running between towels and sheets billowing in the summer breeze. The beating sun acted as a natural bleach for laundry hanging outside, but it had the opposite effect on us—the whiter our shirts and underwear, the darker our skin.

Still, who could resist the gorgeous sun after all that miserable rain? We leaped over croaking frogs to catch dragonflies with our nets. We flew our kites on little dirt trails that meandered through the rice paddies. We stayed active and happy until the sun went down or Mother called us in for dinner, whichever came first.

Speaking of my mother's voice, I loved hearing it—especially when she sang traditional Japanese folk songs. Whenever I came home crying over a scraped knee, my mom rocked me on her lap and sang softly to console me. I was so comforted by her sweet voice that I often pretended to continue crying long after my tears stopped. That was when I learned that music, along with a mother's touch, has miraculous healing power.

When typhoon season began, usually in late August, our summer fun hit a snag. Once again we took shelter in our little Japanese house in Osaka, by now somewhat purged of the mold smell.

And what was our biggest weapon against typhoons? Surprisingly strong aluminum storm shutters.

It always amazed me that such a flimsy thing could hold back major storms. My sisters and I often slid the shutters closed to darken the room for the opening of a show that we wrote, directed, and starred in. In contrast to those ten-minute productions, typhoons were great events of nature produced and directed by God Almighty—and they could last for hours.

Our ice-cube air conditioner was ineffective now; no amount of air movement could counteract the increasing mugginess as the typhoon approached. When storm clouds appeared, the shutters were rolled into place, this time for the real show. The whipping wind rattled the shutters against our glass windows and wooden doors, and our house shook like an imbalanced load of laundry during spin cycle.

Hunkered down on tatami floors, we were sure the entire house would blow away. We sat in our darkened house, flashlights at the ready, the AM radio tuned to the latest report. We passed the time by playing cards and folding more origami paper, shouting to one another over the great banging outside.

If we were lucky, the eye of the storm passed directly over us and we could catch a glimpse of the sun peeking through ominous, churning clouds. We would go outside, let our eyes adjust to the light, and look up to find blue skies overhead. These intermissions were always short, so we wasted no time jumping into the puddles, playing on our wet swing set, and stretching our legs before the second act began.

The storm often continued into the wee hours, long after we had drifted off to sleep on the futon laid out on our tatami floor. When we woke up the next morning, we assessed the damage left by the typhoon—a turned-over dog house, broken pots, a neighbor's bicycle now in our backyard. We found ourselves amazed once again that the aluminum storm shutters had protected us from the ferocious power of nature.

I wasn't afraid of these storms, and I didn't mind the rains too much. It was just part of life in Japan. We used to joke that there was rain every Thursday and an earthquake every other Sunday. What I feared was thunder. When I was a toddler, my mom told me that gorogoro-san ("Mr. Thunder") would come and steal my belly button. I couldn't understand what purpose a belly button collection would serve the great Mr. Thunder, but it sounded like he was angry. I vowed to do everything in my power to keep my belly button intact.

To this day, I'm not sure why my mother used that fear tactic on me. Maybe she wanted me to cover up my midriff to avoid catching a cold. What she didn't count on was how gullible I was, nor how her words would affect me whenever we had a summer storm. When the lightning flashed and the thunder came crashing down, I immediately ran for a closet. I tucked myself into the fetal position, covered my ears, and prayed away gorogoro-san. Sometimes I shook with fear and bit my lip to choke back tears.

After seeing how I reacted to the thunder, Mother tried to explain that she had only been kidding. But it was too late. I was already a believer, and nothing could take away my fear of gorogoro-san. He was mighty, mad, and out to get me and my belly button.

It was during one such summer, when I was eight years old, that my father came home and announced that we were moving to America.

Ever since meeting American GIs stationed in post–WWII Japan, it had been my father's dream to one day live in America. To his way of thinking, America was wealthy, powerful, and victorious. During his days at the university in Osaka, he used to trade American soldiers fresh cigarettes for a lesson in English. He tuned in to the state-run NHK radio station every day to listen to English-language programming.

Because of his outstanding English skills, he was chosen by his company to represent them overseas. He had already been sent to South Africa and the U.S. once. The first time he and my mother left for New York, it was as a family of three; they returned to Osaka a few years later with two more babies. This time, he vowed, the move to the U.S. would be permanent.

My father got rid of all of our belongings except what fit into our brand-new Samsonite suitcases. My parents obtained passports for us and before we knew it, we were bound for New York.

School was not in session at the time, so my sisters and I didn't get a chance to say good-bye to our friends. We were just happy to escape the rain, humidity, and typhoons. We boarded the airplane armed with stacks of brightly colored square papers to fold. It was going to be a long flight across the Pacific.

SUMMER CAMP AND ICE CREAM SOCIALS

Then he said to them all: "Whoever wants to be my disciple
must deny themselves and take up their cross daily and follow me.
For whoever wants to save their life will lose it,
but whoever loses their life for me will save it."

LUKE 9:23–24

Our family's move from New York to Southern California happened during spring break of my fifth grade year. On my first day at Red Hill Elementary School in Tustin, California, my parents took me to the school office. After they enrolled me, I waited nervously for one of my new classmates to come retrieve me. A few minutes later, a girl wearing a Brownie uniform walked in and introduced herself.

"Hi! I'm Danielle, and you're in my class."

As I followed this girl down the hallway to my new classroom, I decided to break the ice. I cleared my throat and tried out my best English phrasing: "Are. You. In. Girl. Scout?"

Danielle turned around and smiled. "Yes, I am."

She understood me, hooray! Despite the fact that I had spent most of my time at P.S. 24 with my Japanese girlfriends chatting in Japanese (Tokyo dialect, of course), I had learned enough English to be understood by my new Californian friend. I was on my own now, without my bilingual Japanese classmates to translate for me. But I had a feeling I was going to be okay here.

FOR THE REST OF FIFTH GRADE, I focused on acquiring friends at Red Hill Elementary School. Sure, there was that embarrassing incident at the school playground involving my Bronx accent, but that was obviously more damaging to my ego than to potential friendship. It was too bad that I had only a few short weeks to get to know them before we ended the school year.

That summer between my fifth and sixth grade years goes on the record as the longest and most boring of my life. There was no summer camp to attend, and I hadn't made enough close friends for sleepovers or other fun summertime activities. My sisters and I just hung out at our new ranch-style Southern California home. Even a backyard pool can lose its appeal when your only playmates are your sisters.

I was never more relieved than the day we started sixth grade. I was once again in the same class as Danielle, but I was also starting to figure out the popularity lay of the land. I learned quickly that Jayme and Judy were definitely at the top of the heap. They were both athletic, smart, blond, and beautiful. Imagine my surprise, then, when they pulled me aside one day to invite me to their church.

I had no idea what "church" meant, but I imagined it was a place similar to the Catholic church in Fujiidera where my parents sent us for some introductory English classes a few weeks before we moved to the States. I don't remember much about that experience except that we had a heated discussion on how to pronounce the word *vase*. Was it "veys" or "vahs"? No one seemed to know for sure, because none of the nuns who taught the classes actually spoke English. They did let us come into mass once, although we were not allowed to participate. I observed with much curiosity as the priest slipped small white wafers into the mouths of my fellow English learners who professed Catholic faith. The sunlight filtering through the stained-glass windows cast colorful shadows onto the pews. It was a very sacred place.

Judy and Jayme tried to explain that their Presbyterian church was not the same thing as a Catholic church. It didn't make any difference to me; I was delighted to be singled out by them, and eager to find out more about church.

So after a sleepover at Jayme's place on Saturday night, I went with them to church the next morning. In Sunday school, I saw a big map on the wall and listened to the teacher, Mrs. Prell, talk about a man named Paul who went on a missionary journey. Apparently Paul had a friend or two join him on occasion, but they were only sidekicks—Paul was the real hero.

I felt like I had walked into the middle of a good movie and everyone except me knew the plot. *Who was this Paul character? What was he doing in such treacherous waters?* I had lots of questions, but they were forgotten when Mrs. Prell brought out vanilla wafers and Dixie cups of apple juice.

Even if we'd skipped that wonderful snack, I was glad to be there. This church thing felt so completely American. Perhaps if I hung around this place long enough, I would eventually become a real American too.

After Sunday school was dismissed, I listened in curiosity to a conversation between Mrs. Prell and her daughter, Wendy.

"I love you, Wendy."

"I love you too, Mom, even though you don't always like me."

"Dear, sometimes I don't like what you are *doing*. But I always love *you!*"

We just didn't talk like that in our home—no one in Japan did! This touchy-feely thing must be yet another aspect of American culture.

I didn't know how I would react if my mom or dad spoke to me like that. *Maybe it would be nice*, I thought, a little envious.

I also noticed that Mrs. Prell had a thick book with pages as thin as rice paper. It must have been thousands of pages long! On just about every page, she had scribbled notes in the margins. To me, this meant she actually read and thought about every word.

I was curious about this book. What was in it that interested Mrs. Prell so much? But I knew it would take me a long time to read it. *Maybe when I'm as old as Mrs. Prell, I'll get to it.*

One Sunday evening a few weeks later, Judy and her family invited me to an ice cream social at the church. After a singalong accompanied by pipe organ and guitar (yes, it was the '70s), we went into the fellowship hall for refreshments. I scooped as much ice cream as I could into my paper bowl, then piled on hot fudge and whipped cream and topped it with sprinkles and nuts.

I sat down with Judy's family to enjoy my creation. At the next table was Jayme, talking and laughing with her parents and siblings. Everywhere there were families; I was the only tagalong.

Someday, I resolved, *I will be at an ice cream social with my own family.*

A couple of months later, Jayme invited me to go with her and her older sister to see a film. She mentioned something about it being a part of a Billy Graham Crusade. I had no idea who this Billy was, but it sounded like fun—I had never seen a movie in a real theater before. Japan didn't have movie theaters like the ones in the States.

We got our popcorn and sat down in the velvet-covered seats. Soon the lights dimmed and the movie began to roll. I don't remember much of it except that it was called *Time to Run* and featured the song "I Love You" by Jesus music pioneer Randy Stonehill. The acting was good, but the dialogue moved too swiftly for my non-native ears to pick up. It was a little like watching a foreign film—without subtitles.

When the lights came back on, Jayme asked if I had liked the movie. Enthusiastically, I replied, "Yes!" I desperately hoped she wouldn't ask what I liked about it.

Then Jayme asked if I wanted to walk to the front of the theater and talk to a counselor about becoming a Christian.

Are you kidding? I thought. *I can become a Christian without having to be born into a Christian family in America? I don't have to be a blond Caucasian to join? I don't have to ask my parents?*

Jayme and her sister introduced me to a kind, middle-aged woman who reminded me of Mrs. Prell. She asked, "Junko, do you know that God loves you?"

If you mean that God loves me the way Jayme, Judy, Mrs. Prell, and everyone at the ice cream social seem to love me... "Yes."

"Do you know that you are sinful?"

Well, we're all human, so I guess so. "Yes."

"Did you know that Jesus died for your sins?"

I think I need more information. No, I'll come back to this later. "Yes."

"Would you like to accept him into your heart?"

Is this the part where I get my membership card? "Of course, yes!"

The counselor had me close my eyes. Jayme and her sister stood close while the counselor prayed with me to accept Jesus into my heart.

When we were done, she gave me a booklet to study and told me about a correspondence course I could join to learn the basics of Christianity. I took the booklet gladly and, before the evening was over, had memorized the first verse:

For God so loved the world that he gave his one and only Son, that whoever believes in him shall not perish but have eternal life. (John 3:16)

I said the verse over and over in my head as we drove home. I was elated to be part of this group that had showered me with such love.

They let me in! I guess I'm good enough, I thought. *It feels good to be accepted and to belong, and I'm going to work hard to study this booklet so that Jayme's family will be proud of my decision to join them.*

Back home, I floated into my house, where my sisters and my parents were engrossed in a television program. When they asked at the commercial break if I'd had a good time, I cleared my throat and announced that I had become a Christian.

My parents looked up at me for a second, at each other, and then back to the TV. My dad said, "Just don't get too deep into that religion stuff."

I assured him that I wouldn't. However, even as I walked toward my bedroom, I had a feeling that this "Christianity thing" was going to demand all of me and then some.

I was ready to dive down deep.

$\mathcal{F}$OR THE REST OF THAT SCHOOL YEAR, I went as often as I could to church with Judy and Jayme. My parents usually didn't object, as they had no particular opinion about Christianity, good or bad. They just knew that my friends were good girls and that it seemed like a safe place for one of their daughters to spend her time.

Besides, they had their hands full with the Japanese restaurant they had opened. Two years after we moved to New York, my dad got orders from his company to return to Japan. Rather than do that, he decided to quit his job. But how would he support his family in this foreign country? That's when he found a business partner in California to open a Japanese restaurant with, which is why we moved to the West Coast.

My parents spent long hours getting the business going, so they could hardly keep track of their daughters' comings and goings. As parents, however, they did want some family time together, so I occasionally missed church out of respect to them—and to help with household chores.

In truth, though, I would have loved to spend every minute of the day at church. Maybe it was the fun group of friends I met there; maybe it was the peace and calm I felt at church in comparison to the stress I felt at home while my parents worked overtime to provide for us. Whatever the case, something drew my heart strongly to church and to…well, perhaps God? Although to my twelve-year-old way of thinking, God and church were sort of separate entities. I tried to pay attention during Sunday school, but I still didn't comprehend everything. As a result, I didn't learn a lot more about God after my initial introduction at the movie theater with Jayme.

Part of the problem was that I didn't read or study the Bible very much. I just liked holding it and carrying it around with me; it sort of made me feel holy. Nonetheless, I knew that church was a place where it was safe to be myself, and that was very appealing to me. And it beat cleaning windows and vacuuming the carpet, hands down!

ONE SATURDAY AFTERNOON IN MAY, JUST BEFORE the end of sixth grade in Southern California, my friend Judy and her mom stopped by my house to talk to my parents about letting me go to junior high camp that summer at a nearby Christian conference center.

While Judy and I chased each other in my backyard, her mom took the time to describe for my parents—in slow, clear English—a camp called Forest Home in the San Bernardino Mountains.

I suspected that my parents would let me go; they knew how much I loved summer camp from the two I had attended in the Catskills, shortly after we moved to New York. Sure enough, without hesitation, my mom wrote the check that day and signed the permission slip.

A few weeks later I boarded a bus in the church parking lot, my arms laden with my sleeping bag and pillow and my heart filled with excitement. A little over an hour later, we arrived at Forest Home.

The air was crisp and dry, and we jockeyed for the top bunk in our cabins as we began a week in what I thought was the closest place to heaven on earth. (It's a mile closer, in fact.) We sang silly songs at the top of our lungs as the talented and handsome youth leader led us on the guitar. We went horseback riding and hiking in the hills, we swam, and we laughed until our sides hurt.

This was a lot like the camp in the Catskill Mountains but even better, for it was church every night! I believed that I belonged there. I had made the decision just a few weeks earlier to gain my membership into this nice group of people. But I still didn't know what the membership meant.

At the campfire one night during the week, the good-looking youth leader asked all the campers, "Do you know that God loves you?"

God loves us? Hmmm.

I knew God existed. I was sure that only someone as powerful as God could create typhoons, give us the sun and the rain, and, most importantly, give me life. But I also assumed that this God was at best indifferent, and at worst angry. After all, I was sure that the same God who created the universe took on the form of gorogoro-san during thunderstorms and was out to get me.

And it sure seemed that whenever I did something bad, like being sassy to my mother, something went wrong right away. Often within minutes, for instance, I'd trip and scrape my knees, and that was pretty much the only time the thought of a Supreme Being would pop in my head: I commit a transgression, then God punishes me. During some of the thunderstorms back in Japan, as I cowered with fear, I mentally reviewed all my actions leading up to that afternoon, wondering which transgression was offensive enough to anger gorogoro-san, thus resulting in this punishment. No wonder! It never dawned on me that this God would actually care about me and love me. I knew that the *people* of God were loving and accepting of me, but God himself? Well…

(I know, you must be wondering how it is that after spending all that time at church, I still didn't get it. In spite of the fact that at one point I learned—at least in theory—that God is not the angry Mr. Thunder I heard about as a child, I still confused the two in my mind. In hindsight, I blame that on not ever cracking open the Bible Judy's mom gave me and learning about the true God firsthand, but instead continuing to rely on my childhood impressions of him.)

"You are a sinful person, and you are far separated from him," the youth leader went on.

There you go! See, I knew I was a bad little girl. Yes, I am always angering this God. That's why I cowered in fear and hid from him just as I always had from Mr. Thunder.

"But God sent his only Son, Jesus Christ, to this world so that he could pay the penalty for your sins. If you confess your sins and trust in him, then you too will be forgiven." I was very glad the youth leader had kept talking.

So that's what it meant to be a Christian—to be forgiven and to have a restored relationship with this God. *I'm all for that! Yes, I want to be forgiven! I don't want to keep running away from God—and I want my belly button intact!*

"We're going to pray now, and if you want to have a relationship with Christ and accept Jesus into your heart, then slip your hand up so I can see you."

I had already done this at the movie theater with Jayme. But just in case I somehow messed it up the first time, I quietly raised my hand. I wanted to guarantee a relationship with God.

"Thank you. And thank *you*," he said. "Yes, you in the back, thank you. Is there anyone else? Thank you. I see your hand. Anyone else want to? Yes, thank you."

It seemed like a busy night. I was surprised so many Americans weren't Christians yet.

"When you are forgiven, it's like you were covered in dirt, you jumped into a beautiful lake, and you came out completely clean. God washes away all your sins, and he cleanses you until your heart is sparkling clean and pure white. As white as snow."

Whew! I knew how it felt to be dirty and how good it felt to be clean again after a nice warm bath. But I couldn't kick the nagging feeling that no matter how hard I scrubbed, my skin would never be as clean as my Caucasian friends sitting around me.

I would be as clean as I could be, I supposed, and that's pretty good for a Japanese girl.

After we returned to our cabin, the skies started to rumble and rain began to fall. A summer storm was rolling in. Tossing and turning in my sleeping bag, I tried to ignore the thunder and lightning. I reminded myself that I was safe. I shared the cabin with six girls and a counselor who all loved and accepted me. I also reviewed my day's transgressions and confessed each one. I felt at peace.

As I drifted off to sleep, I laced my fingers over my belly button— just in case.

INTRO TO MUSIC

Sing to him a new song; play skillfully,
and shout for joy.

PSALM 33:3

Like almost every little Japanese girl, I began taking classical piano lessons in the first grade. This continued for two years, until we moved to New York. In the Bronx we didn't have a piano in our apartment, so I gave up my lessons—but not my desire to learn. At school I tried to befriend girls who had pianos in their homes so I could sneak in some time on the ivory keys during our play dates.

When we moved into our California house a few years later, I was delighted to find that the previous owner had left her piano behind. Now I could play at home! After stocking up on songbooks of popular music and Broadway hits, I continued my self-directed quest to learn the piano. They say that practice makes perfect, but in actuality practice makes permanent. Despite my good intentions, I only reinforced poor technique.

Then one afternoon during seventh grade, while I was digging for more music at Wynn's Music Store, I met Rich Briggs.

Rich taught piano in one of the private classrooms at the back of the store. He could play bass, drums, keyboard, and guitar as well as piano. He also wrote, arranged, and produced music. His many career achievements even included music director for Richard Simmons's exercise videos!

I filled him in on my situation, and Rich immediately took me back to the basics. One sonata at a time, he corrected my fingering and note reading. Every week I rode my bike to Wynn's, determined to make up for years spent teaching myself to play the piano and consequently developing bad habits.

Two years into my lessons with him, Rich surprised me with the declaration, "I can't teach you any more about piano playing. If you want to improve technically as a pianist, Junko, you need to get yourself another teacher, because you've reached my limit." A trumpet blared through the thin wood paneling separating our lesson room from the next as Rich continued, "But if you want to learn about pop music—about playing by ear, improvising, and songwriting—then I'm your guy."

Pop music and songwriting? That's exactly what I wanted!

Without hesitation, I signed on to continue with Rich. And that is how I entered the fascinating world of pop music. It was my first step toward fulfilling a dream I had had since I was a little girl running around in Osaka.

AT AGE SEVEN, I JUST *knew* I was going to be a professional musician. Talk about the hubris of youth!

Sure, I started playing piano at an early age, but I was hardly a

prodigy. Now take my friend and producer John Andrew Schreiner—
he's a prodigy. By age five he was performing on TV; at eighteen he
was producing music. And he also has perfect pitch!

Yes, I loved to sing, but the best you could say about me was that
I sang mostly on pitch and, like my mother, had a pure voice.

Convinced that I was going to be a star someday, I knew it would
be important to have original material. I wrote my first song in second grade. It was for a contest at the Fujiidera elementary school;
students were asked to submit lyrics for the new school anthem, and
of course I chose to compete. I walked around all day humming the
melody and came up with a set of lyrics I thought were pretty good.
I ended up winning the second-grade submissions and ultimately
came in second to a sixth grader in the schoolwide competition. I
loved that sweet taste of success.

I also knew it was important to study vocals, so I listened intently
to people singing on TV and radio and tried to mimic every nuance
and intonation. American music was just as popular in Japan during
the '60s as it was everywhere else in the world. To this day, when I
hear Simon & Garfunkel, I am transported to the home of my mom's
cousins. Mother grew up at their home in Toyonaka after she lost
her parents during the war. She was only fourteen when her uncle
took her and her brothers in. By the time I came along, her young-
est cousin was still a teenager. During our visits, he would blast the
Beatles and Bob Dylan on his AM radio while we played on their
tatami floor. During one of these visits, I noticed how professional
singers held their long notes with a vibrato. I didn't have a vibrato;
I always sang my notes straight. I tried and tried to reproduce the
same sound, but I simply warbled.

It wasn't until years later, when I was in high school, that I found
my vibrato. I was taking private voice lessons from the school music

teacher, Mr. Ed Doyle. He had me lie on the ground and breathe so I would know where my diaphragm was. He also had me sing "ahhh" while going up and down half-step intervals, speeding up the movement until I produced a true vibrato.

Although Mr. Doyle has passed on, I still thank him whenever I hold out my long notes. More importantly, I thank him for being one of the key people to believe in my potential as a singer and musician. I started as an accompanist for his elite Madrigals choir; by the end of my senior year, I was one of his regular soloists.

ALMOST EVERYONE RECALLS THE FIRST album they ever purchased. Mine was *Tapestry* by Carole King. Talk about great songwriting! When she sang "I feel the earth move under my feet," she expressed exactly how I felt about that blond-haired boy, Michael, in my fourth-grade class on whom I had a terrible crush. And when I looked in the mirror while she sang "You're beautiful as you feel," I felt that I just might be the world's prettiest nine-year-old…until the song's end, of course.

King's arrangements were simple by today's standards, but each of her well-crafted songs offered a three-minute escape from routine—which included, at the time, my homework and wishing I could go back to Osaka. Our apartment in New York was a high-rise in a complex of several buildings which all looked exactly the same. I used to stare out the window at the red bricks covering the building next to ours and wish so much that I were seeing sprawling rice fields instead. If I closed my eyes and imagined hard enough, I could almost hear my friend Yukako stopping by my house with her own kite calling out, "*Asobimasho!* Come out and play!" Nothing could take away that longing I felt to go home, save for some great Carole

King, James Taylor, and Jackson 5 tunes which soothed the pain, even for a little while.

*A*S EARLY AS ELEMENTARY SCHOOL, I figured out that a good pop song is made up of the following components: a compelling melody, great lyrics, and a predictable pattern that goes verse, chorus, verse, chorus, bridge (sometimes instrumental), chorus, then fade.

I really wanted to sing along with *Tapestry*, Jackson 5, James Taylor, and the Beatles. The trouble was, I still lacked English-speaking skills. To me, the lyrics of any song were simply a string of syllables and sounds without much meaning.

When I was in third grade, our class learned a song for Back-to-School Night. It started out, "Mommy told me something..." Those were the only words I knew until we got to the chorus: "So let the sunshine in"—only to my foreign ears, it sounded like, "So *there's still some Chinese*." Why were we singing to our parents about some Chinese? I wondered. I hummed along and mumbled my way through the song as best I could, hiding behind my monotone classmates and searching for my parents in the sea of smiling faces.

The following year, the fourth-grade classes at P.S. 24 decided to do an abridged production of *Fiddler on the Roof* during the spring semester. I wanted so badly to audition. But try as I might, I could not memorize or even sing the lyrics. So the main parts went to boys and girls who could barely carry a tune, and it nearly killed me. I dutifully sang in the chorus.

But one day my voice caught my teacher's ears. She had everyone stop so she could hear me sing the phrase again by myself. I'm sure I butchered the words, but it was my shining moment. The teacher said something to me that I didn't understand, but the look on her face offered the encouragement I needed.

I AM NOT THE FIRST PERSON IN MY family tree with a seed of musical talent. Back in her day, my great-grandmother was a pop star in Kobe, Japan. I discovered this as an adult. Turns out that around the turn of the century—and I mean from the nineteenth to the twentieth century—a young professional singer named Jiu (pronounced *jee*-ooh) had developed quite a following among the college-age and young adult crowds. Jiu's specialty was a mix of the folk songs and ballads popular in Japan at the time. She often sang at clubs in the area where the many sailors in that port town congregated. She was also hired frequently to sing at local Buddhist temples for various occasions.

Jiu's biggest fan was Mr. Hori, a local businessman who built a successful company painting the exteriors of ships, many of which sailed across the sea to bring back goods from abroad. By the time he met Jiu, Mr. Hori had traveled extensively, a fact which undoubtedly helped impress her enough to marry him. A bit of an amateur musician himself, he liked to accompany his new bride on *shamisen*, a traditional Japanese stringed instrument. My mother recalls attending one of their concerts at their big mansion when she was a young girl growing up in Kobe. Before they lost everything in the war, my great-grandparents had enough money to employ several servants in their home and lavish their grandkids with gifts.

An even more notable example of musical talent in my family is Yoko Narahashi. Yoko is an Academy Award–winning film producer (*The Last Samurai*) as well as former manager and songwriter for Godiego, one of the top bands in Japan during the 1980s. Yoko's parents are my mom's cousins, which makes her my first cousin twice removed. (Or is that my second cousin once removed?) She and my mom were close in age and played together as kids; my mother even named my older sister after her.

One more thing about that family tree…. It dawned on me one day that my great-grandmother Jiu was, at the time and in her way, a "church singer" like I am now. Granted, she sang at Buddhist temples and I sing at Christian churches, but similarities do exist. I wish I could have sat in the audience with my mom at that mansion during one of her neighborhood concerts.

And Jiu probably started out singing at weddings and funerals, just like I did. I wonder how she felt when she made cold calls for bookings, if her heart danced when she got an important gig, whether she ever entered vocal competitions, what she did for warm-up exercises. When did she realize she had a gift? What did her voice sound like? I wonder if she loved the stage the first time she stepped onto it, just as I did at my first piano recital in second grade.

WHEN PEOPLE ASK IF I HAVE A DEGREE in music, I have to say no.

I answer with more than a little embarrassment. My degree is in computer science from UC Irvine. I was trying to be a responsible Asian girl, so I chose a career path that would somewhat guarantee me employment after graduation. The funny thing is that I know many fellow engineers and programmers who are also musicians. I know God created both the logical and creative minds, and I find it fascinating that he fuses both sides of the brain together in music.

What I *should* tell people, though, is that I am a proud graduate of the Rich Briggs Conservatory of Music. For starters, I had to pass Rich's Music Theory 101.

Rich taught me all about chords and how to build C, F, G, and the like. I was studying geometry at the time, and I was fascinated by the parallels I observed between music and geometry.

Rich also taught me to play by ear. He and I would listen to a song, paying careful attention to the bass line; this helped define the key as well as the chord progressions. Most of the time, I discovered, pop songs have very predictable chord progressions (such as I, IV, V, I or I, VI, IV, V, for those of you who know what I'm talking about), so they were fairly easy to figure out.

Jazz tunes were more difficult. Once, Rich had me listen to an Oscar Peterson recording so I could play along with this jazz great. I was able to hang in there with Oscar for about eight bars until he started improvising like a butterfly in a garden. By contrast, I was more like a barely moving caterpillar.

That was my first exposure to jazz improvisation, which I appreciate but does not come naturally to me. Rich could tickle the ivory and do all the jazz licks with his fingers just like Oscar Peterson, but I was a stiff-fingered eighth grader in awe that a human being could actually do that. Deciding I was not cut out for jazz, I continued to pour my energy into pop music.

Next, Rich issued the challenge of songwriting. My assignment was to listen to top hits at the time and bring back an analysis of one the following week. I think I listened to songs by Elton John or James Taylor and returned the next lesson with my treasure map: a lead sheet scribbled with chords and lyrics, highlighting the most intriguing parts of his song. The chord progression, the catchy melody, and even the arrangements and orchestrations were clues leading us to the holy grail of songwriting: a number one hit on the Billboard charts.

My next assignment was to copy—ahem, borrow—some of the best elements of the song and come up with my own. And that's when I learned that the music portion of songwriting was the easy part for me; lyrics were a different story.

By now I was much more proficient in my English and could converse pretty well. I no longer spoke with an accent, and I was even pulling pretty decent grades in school. However, writing lyrics in English required me to dip into an area of my brain that had never before been used for that purpose.

Actually, let me rephrase that. That area of the brain had helped me win the school anthem competition in second grade, but that meant it was *occupied by a different language*. After coming to this country, I simply could not understand the lyrics to most songs on the radio. As a result, I fell into the habit of not really listening to them. I tuned out the words and focused on the music. Except for the catchy hook (usually the most-repeated line of the chorus), the lyrics became a blur.

That's why I was surprised to learn from Rich that for most people, the lyrics—*not* the music—are the more meaningful part of a song. For me, a song was all about the music! I might as well have been listening only to instrumental numbers. If you don't know what I mean, next time you eat at an Italian, Indian, or other ethnic restaurant that is playing authentic music from that culture, try listening and see if you don't also tune out the words after a while.

But back to Rich's challenge. I tried and tried to write lyrics, but they all came out jumbled, nonsensical, just plain dumb. I could craft a compelling melody, something I might actually enjoy singing; but I had a classic case of writer's block.

The following week, I showed Rich my instrumental piece and tearfully explained my dilemma. He laughed, patted me on the back, and told me to relax and keep writing.

His response was the encouragement I needed. I went home, sat down at the piano, and started working on a new song. But this time, instead of pausing to edit each phrase, I let words flow in large chunks. They weren't exactly "deep" lyrics, but they rhymed okay and were occasionally silly and actually fun.

This freedom—knowing it was okay just to try something, anything—allowed me to experiment and actually be productive. Rich was as surprised as I when I showed up the following week with a complete song.

Now, whenever I hit writer's block, I think about Rich's advice to stop editing and critiquing before I'm done writing. Just write—then go back to edit.

At last I had found my own holy grail—the art of songwriting. I may never achieve that Billboard top hit, but it brings me great pleasure to have listeners tell me they can't get one of my songs out of their head. "It's making me crazy!" they'll say. I apologize for the crazy part, but inside I am overjoyed.

"Be Ye Perfect"

*You, therefore, must be perfect [growing into complete maturity of
godliness in mind and character, having reached the proper height
of virtue and integrity], as your heavenly Father is perfect.*

Matthew 5:48, AMP

After my experience at Forest Home summer camp, I
pursued my new faith with the determination of a
born perfectionist. I didn't miss a single junior-high
activity at Trinity United Presbyterian Church. I attended youth
group on Sundays, Bible study on Tuesdays, choir on Wednesdays,
pool & BBQ time on Fridays, and outreach projects on Saturdays. I
felt guilty if I missed an event and prayed that the Lord would forgive me for my absence.

But my devotion to these activities wasn't prompted by guilt; I
was going because I *enjoyed* them. Every one.

Steve Yamaguchi, my first youth leader, was a Japanese American
who even spoke a little Japanese! God was definitely a step ahead of
me. Steve was a student at Westmont College in Santa Barbara, and

he was serving as the interim junior high director when I showed up one Sunday. I was pretty much in awe of him.

Steve planned all sorts of activities for us junior highers, but the one I remember best was the day we spent fishing at Newport Pier. My parents dropped me off at the church parking lot around 7 a.m. The Southern California marine layer known as June Gloom clouded the skies, but it could not dampen my enthusiasm.

For some reason, the only other kid to show up that day was a boy named Jeff. I didn't mind. Jeff was nice and also kind of cute, and I would have him all to myself! Of course, in typical junior-high fashion, I waved hello, he said hi, and that was pretty much the extent of our conversation for the day.

Steve drove us to the beach in the church van, and we spent all morning fishing. Actually, it would be more truthful to say that we *tried* fishing because neither Steve nor I caught a thing. Jeff did catch a very small fish—and, following the rules, promptly threw it back in.

When we returned to the church a few hours later, Steve led us in a short Bible study. I don't recall what Bible passage he taught from; either my English was still lacking or I was too busy gazing at Jeff (more likely). My parents picked me up just as the June Gloom gave way to the summer sun at high noon.

It had been a wonderful morning.

I recently talked to Pastor Steve about that excursion, which he recalls very differently. He told me how desperate he felt as his carefully laid plans fell apart. First, only two kids showed up. Then he was frustrated by the lack of fish. His Bible study was about how Jesus was the fisher of men, and he had planned to use our fishing expedition as an illustration. So that didn't work. To this young, insecure college student, just trying his best to do this summer job, the whole morning was a disaster.

I was oblivious to Steve's very human emotions because I was having a blast. It didn't matter that we caught zero fish or that the fishing trip didn't support the point of the Bible study; that morning was one of the most significant experiences of my youth. I so appreciate that a godly man like Steve took time to hang out with two awkward junior highers. From my vantage point, it was the perfect day.

And in fact, Steve did catch a fish—me. I was hooked.

"WELCOME TO OUR SMALL GROUP," SAID Lesley Paul as I walked into her parents' sprawling California ranch–style home with its swimming pool in the backyard.

Lesley had just graduated from the same school I would attend, Foothill High School, where she was senior class president, homecoming queen, and yearbook editor. I had scoped out my older sister's copy of that yearbook, and it was amazing. Anything Lesley did turned to gold. She was so mature for her age! I wanted to be just like her.

And now this very busy college-bound young woman was sharing one evening a week teaching us about God's Word. I don't recall missing a single meeting with Lesley and the circle of friends that summer.

By this time, a few other girls were new to the church, so I felt less conspicuous about my lack of Bible knowledge. I still hadn't read that thick book from start to finish like Mrs. Prell had, but I was eager to soak up whatever Lesley taught.

Most of our studies came from the New Testament, and we spent extra time studying some of Paul's epistles—Galatians, Ephesians, Philippians, and Colossians. Then, when we got to Matthew, the opening verse jumped straight out at me.

Be perfect, therefore, as your heavenly Father is perfect.
(Matthew 5:48)

I knew all about perfection. If I worked really hard, I would eventually achieve it. Right? And look—the Bible even told me so! At that point in my young life, the world as I understood it was very simple: you do something good, and you are rewarded. You do something bad, and you are punished. There was no middle ground. I did not want to be punished, so I was going to do all I could to be good.

From that day forward, I was on a quest for perfection. I wanted my heavenly Father to be pleased with me. I didn't want to disappoint him or get on his bad side. Although this desire was well intentioned, it set me on a difficult course.

My desire to be perfect in God's eyes started with getting good grades. My husband's nephew, a professor at a community college with a high Asian population, jokingly refers to Bs as "Asian Fail." Indeed, anything other than an A was unacceptable to me, and I was sure God felt the same way.

As soon as my English was proficient enough, I began to earn my As at school. I did especially well in math, entering several math contests around town and bringing home trophies. Even in my worst subjects, history and English, I could earn good grades if I worked really, really hard. So work hard, I did.

But I wanted to excel at all aspects of school, not just academics. I ran for various student body offices, serving as vice president of my junior high school, class president my junior year, and pep commissioner my senior year. I don't think I ever lost an election, mainly because I always did my research ahead of time to make certain I had a good chance of winning. Only then would I declare my candidacy. Frankly, my motivation for running for office did not come from any interest in school politics; getting elected was just a way to boost my ego.

I was also quite involved in music during high school. I worked my way up from being just a singer in the freshman choir to accompanying and singing solos in the Madrigals choir. I received the school's music award my senior year.

Still, academics, student government, and fine arts weren't enough. I tried out for various sports, but quickly discovered the limits of my athleticism in any sport involving equipment.

You see, when I wasn't good at something right from the start, I quickly sidestepped it. I wanted to be perceived as perfect, so I only did things I was good at.

I ended up running cross country, mostly because I figured out that running was a way to burn calories. Being thin had become increasingly important as I approached my senior year. I wasn't fast, but I had endurance—a quality that served me well in cross country and life in general.

Cross country is not a glamorous sport, so the cheerleading squad was reluctant to come cheer at cross country and track meets. We had a strong team of runners, however, and the coach demanded that the squad send over at least a few cheerleaders at the league finals that we were sure to win.

As pep commissioner, my job was to assign the cheerleaders to various events. That day I ran with my cross country team, quickly changed into my pep commissioner uniform, and hurried over with my pom-poms to hand out medals and orange slices. I was a busy girl.

I was voted onto the homecoming court, named Most Talented in the yearbook, and graduated high school with several awards and scholarships. I wasn't quite a Lesley, but if I do say so myself, I was doing pretty darn well—and I was sure God was pleased with me.

I was so busy accomplishing things that I wasn't even aware of one very significant difference between Lesley and me. Lesley's accomplishments were fueled by a quiet strength that came from deep within, a strength that grew out of her relationship with God. Mine came from a stormy place hidden underneath my happy-go-lucky exterior. It would take years to recognize and understand the difference between Lesley's strength and my storm.

BY THE TIME I GRADUATED FROM HIGH school, I had almost forgotten I was Japanese. My English didn't have an obvious accent, so most kids had no idea I had been in this country for less than ten years and that I wasn't fluent before junior high.

I still lacked a broad vocabulary. To hide this in conversation, I let other people do the talking while I smiled and nodded. Most people, I found, like to hear themselves talk. By letting them do so, I gained more friends and became more popular. It was an easy gig.

There was not a single other Japanese-speaking student at my high school besides my sisters and me, so I actually started to forget my Japanese. My kite-flying days in the rice fields seemed like a lifetime ago. I now marched into my friends' homes wearing my shoes without even thinking twice about it. My thoughts were preoccupied by the same things as any typical Southern California teenage girl: boys, fashion, food, youth group, popularity, movies, and college.

Asians jokingly refer to people like me as "bananas": yellow on the outside, white on the inside. I had assimilated quite well into the American culture.

But deep inside I was still the frightened little girl who had just arrived in this country. A little girl puzzled and overwhelmed by all the new things that came her way. Even the busyness of high school and the rush of my achievements couldn't mask my unease. Whenever I slowed down, I would start to think, *Maybe I'm not good enough. Maybe I'm still too, you know, "different." Maybe God isn't quite pleased with me. Maybe I need to be more perfect.*

*I*N THE FALL OF 1979, I STARTED college at UC Irvine. That huge campus, with its student population of over twenty thousand, was about ten times bigger than my high school. Lectures were often filled with hundreds of students, all cream-of-the-crop graduates from their respective high schools.

In comparison to these academic stars, I was just average. Mind you, average at a major university like UC Irvine is not bad. But I could not handle the fact that I was not at the top.

This was when I realized that I lacked good study habits. In high school, I coasted by on memorization skills rather than critical thinking or analytical ability. But high school is not as rigorous as college and certainly not as rigorous as UCI. I was required to take humanities classes that introduced me to classic literature and great thinkers in history—and I actually needed to *study* for those classes. I had to write essays on social and political matters that I cared not one iota about.

I tried to focus on the professor's lectures, but I never had a clue what he was talking about. What did Alexis de Tocqueville's nineteenth-century writings have to do with my life today? It's amazing that I didn't fail any of my classes that first year. Actually, I barely got by. Falling short of perfection like this was very disturbing to me.

And academia was not the only source of my discomfort. In an effort to save money, I commuted to UCI my freshman year instead of living in the dorms. While new roommates laughed and got to know one another over lunch in the cafeteria, I sat by myself, looking for someone—anyone—to talk to.

Even worse, my car was not very reliable, so I sometimes took the bus. With its circuitous routes and transfers, a bus adventure could turn my twenty-minute car drive into a couple of hours. On those days I had to cart all of my heavy books in my green backpack to every class, then turn around and take the long bus ride home.

And there was more culture shock in store. In high school, everyone knew my name; at UC Irvine, I was a student ID number. No one noticed if I came or went.

I was invited to join Inter-Varsity Christian Fellowship and went to a few meetings, but living off-campus made it difficult to attend many activities. Besides, Inter-Varsity wasn't like my beloved high school youth group. Unfortunately, going back to my church wasn't fun either, because most of my good friends had gone away to college.

I had a disturbing feeling of being left behind. It seemed like everything in my life was different.

I tried to study—or rather, learn to study—but my grades kept slipping. I had never seen a C before in my life; now they were popping up everywhere. It was even worse than Asian Fail! The harder I tried and the more I studied, the more my grades seemed to head south.

For the first time, just working really, really hard wasn't enough. I was sure that I was disappointing God with my low grades, my spotty church attendance, and my lack of making friends.

College life improved a bit my sophomore year, when I moved into the dorms. At least then I could make friends and attend on-campus activities with Inter-Varsity. I became a little more adept at college-level thinking in my humanities courses, and I began to take math- and computer science–related classes for my major, classes that I found more tolerable than those abstract humanities courses. I like things black and white, and at its core, that's what computer science is all about: bits on or bits off, true or false. There are no gray areas in math or computers.

Even as I became more comfortable at UCI, my pursuit of perfection did not let up. But finding myself less and less effective in achieving academic perfection, I poured my energy into my running.

I'd go out for four, five, or six miles almost every day—I loved the endorphin high it gave me. However, I managed to turn even this leisure activity into something stressful by trying to increase my weekly mileage and better my time with each run. I became enslaved to running.

I entered local 5K and 10K races and did pretty well—but I was not satisfied if I didn't better my personal record time at the next race. At first it was easy to see improvements, because I started out a very slow runner and moved up to being just a normal slow runner. I eventually became somewhat fast, but that's when I hit the limits of my God-given talent. From there, my performance plateaued.

This was symbolic of my life: I would initially excel at whatever endeavor I pursued until I hit a ceiling. After that point, the harder I tried, the more elusive any improvement became. My natural response was to try even harder. I refused to let myself think about the diminishing returns of my efforts.

SOMETIME IN THE SPRING OF MY SECOND year at college, something happened that changed my life. I came across a small book with an intriguing title: *Your God Is Too Small*, by J. B. Phillips.

It was all about the misconceptions we have of God, including the view I held—God the Perfectionist.

As I read, I came to understand that although God is perfect, he does not expect perfection out of us. Talk about a giant relief! I didn't have to become perfect by my own strength. In fact, if I *could* achieve perfection on my own, I would have no need for a Savior.

> It is by grace you have been saved, through faith—and this
> is not from yourselves, it is the gift of God—not by works,
> so that no one can boast. (Ephesians 2:8–9)

I had discovered the whole point of the gospel of Jesus Christ. *Why hadn't I seen it before?*

I'm certain that this truth was taught at my church, but I wasn't listening. I had grown accustomed to tuning out sermons and lectures, a carryover of the same habit I developed before I understood English. Whenever I got lost, I would gloss over my teacher's words or the lyrics of a song. Even when I was hearing, I was not truly listening.

I used this same habit of selective listening to support my conception of God. When I ran across verses like "Love one another" (John 13:34) or "Do not conform any longer to the pattern of this world, but be transformed by the renewing of your mind" (Romans 12:2), I turned them into legalistic commands.

In my heart, I was not truly grateful. I did things in the name of Christian duty and obligation rather than out of a heartfelt sense of gratitude. *Why would God give me even more things to do on my already full plate?* I wondered. *Isn't he satisfied with me yet?* My Christian walk was not a walk of joy; it was a to-do list I could never completely accomplish.

I spent the next few weeks slowly unwinding the tape in my head that had constantly played the "you're not good enough" message for the last several years.

I am good enough, darn it, because God made me this way. I don't have to be perfect in my own power. Now I can truly live!

I started reading the Bible and listening to sermons with a whole new understanding. This time, God's Word, the sermons I heard, and the Christian books I read made sense. It was as if the scales had fallen off my eyes and I could see clearly.

I am reminded of the story about Jesus healing the blind man in Bethsaida:

> Some people brought a blind man and begged Jesus to touch him. He took the blind man by the hand and led him outside the village. When he had spit on the man's eyes and put his hands on him, Jesus asked, "Do you see anything?"
>
> He looked up and said, "I see people; they look like trees walking around."
>
> Once more Jesus put his hands on the man's eyes. Then his eyes were opened, his sight was restored, and he saw everything clearly. (Mark 8:22–25)

I often wondered why it took two tries for Jesus to heal this man. Couldn't the first try have been perfectly effective? Why did Jesus have to use spit at all, as if his saliva has magical powers? I really have no definitive explanation, but it was encouraging for me to see that healing can come in stages.

Similarly, we may not fully grasp a concept the first time we hear it. Perhaps it takes another hearing—or more—to arrive at true knowledge of a verse or a biblical teaching.

At first my understanding of Christ was incomplete, just as the partially healed, formerly blind man initially mistook blurry trees for people. Once his sight was fully restored, he saw objects much more clearly. It took me seven years and a whole lot of wasted energy, emotional and physical, to reach that point of seeing God's truth clearly and accurately.

Thankfully, in God's good timing and by his grace, I came to understand that his grace covers me. At last I could see why Christians say they've been "set free." I was finally free of bondage to perfectionism.

Yes, I am still pretty much a type A personality today. But I have learned to release a lot of things into my heavenly Father's care.

FOR THE FIRST TIME, I UNDERSTOOD THAT theology—my understanding of God—shapes every aspect of my life. My choices, thought patterns, decisions, sicknesses, and a host of other things are affected by how I view God.

In my mind, God was indeed too small. He was my perfectionistic boss, either happy with me when I did well or upset with me when I failed; there was no middle ground. But I was merely projecting my own life philosophy onto a "god" I created in my head. This false god had lost his grip on me, and now I could come out of hiding. Now I could quit protecting my belly button during a thunderstorm!

I no longer had to strive. That truth was incredibly freeing.

Although I tell people that I accepted Christ into my heart when I was in junior high, my walk with God actually began during my second year in college. That was when I discovered God's free gift of grace.

I thought back to my time with Rich Briggs when I was trying so hard to write my first song. Just as I felt relief after Rich patted me on the back and encouraged me to ease up on myself, I felt free after God gave me a pat on the back and a hug to help me stop beating myself up, to help me start breathing and really live.

That pat on the back—the reassurance that came with my correct understanding of God's grace—influenced every area of my life.

For starters, I took up tennis. Yes, this needs-to-always-be-good-at-everything person tried something new that didn't come easily—and still doesn't. I'm not very good at tennis, but I can actually have fun playing tennis now. Missing a serve or not returning one doesn't make me less valuable in God's eyes or anyone else's.

I also found myself able to forgive people, including myself. I didn't feel let down by people as often as I had before. I could tolerate my own mistakes.

Learning about grace with my heart, not just my head, was a gradual process. Reading *Your God Is Too Small* was a turning point, though: it helped me learn to live in God's grace and extend it to others as well as myself.

Curiously, around this time of my awakening to God's grace, I received a flyer in the mail. It was from UC Irvine's Education Abroad Program inviting me to apply for a one-year study abroad program.

Listed as one of the possible destinations: Tokyo, Japan.

God was preparing me to step into my next adventure, a year of living abroad as an exchange student...in my own homeland.

6

HOMEWARD BOUND

*Therefore you are no longer outsiders (exiles, migrants, and aliens,
excluded from the rights of citizens), but you now share citizenship with
the saints (God's own people, consecrated and set apart for Himself);
and you belong to God's [own] household.*

EPHESIANS 2:19, AMP

Welcome to Japan! read the big sign that greeted us at Narita Airport outside Tokyo.

It was June 1981. We were a group of students from several University of California campuses, all on the one-year Education Abroad Program.

I applied after finding out that tuition costs were the same as if I stayed at my home campus and that all the units I took abroad counted toward my UC Irvine credits. In my proud parents' opinion, the additional expenses for travel and living were worth the cost. I was almost as excited as my parents when I received the acceptance letter.

I would be returning to my homeland for the first time since 1969.

I attended orientation meetings during spring quarter but didn't meet my study-abroad classmates until we converged for departure at Los Angeles International Airport. Some were Japanese American, some were white, and some were mixed-blood Eurasians; everyone was enthusiastic about studying in Japan.

These college students had chosen to study in Japan because they were interested in learning about Japanese language and culture. On the plane, I excitedly told them what I remembered about my own country. Never mind that I hadn't thought about some of these things in over a decade! No one else in the group had spent as much time in Japan as I had, so they were eager to learn from me. Some actually knew quite a bit of the language, but no one else spoke it as their mother tongue.

Ever since receiving the mailer for this study abroad program, I could hardly contain my excitement about going back to Japan. For twelve years in America, I had always felt like an alien living in a foreign land. Even when I mastered English, I still looked different from most of my friends, a fact I could not ignore regardless of how well I assimilated into American culture.

I couldn't wait to go back to my own country, to the place where I really belonged. For once, I would be part of the majority. I could almost hear Simon & Garfunkel blaring on the radio at my relatives' home in Toyonaka, Osaka: I was "Homeward Bound"!

FIRST WE ATTENDED AN INTENSIVE six-week language course at International Christian University in Mitaka, Japan, just outside Tokyo. Established about a hundred years ago, ICU is one of the most famous liberal arts colleges in Japan. Many well-known actors and singers attend college there, and it is understood that if you want to learn to speak English while living in Japan, you go to ICU.

A lot of foreign students attended ICU, thereby offering the Japanese students a good exposure to foreign cultures and native English without leaving the country. The University of California campuses all had reciprocal exchange programs with ICU, as did Harvard and several other prestigious institutions around the globe, so I was in fine company with students from a variety of universities.

At our pre-departure orientation, the counselors had repeatedly warned us about culture shock and offered coping tactics should it strike. Me? Oh, I knew about culture shock all right! I had been traumatized by it as a third grader, and I still hadn't quite gotten over it. I hoped the other students would have an easier time with it than I had. Feeling it my duty to make sure my travel companions were prepared for the changes they would face when our plane landed, I liberally dispensed advice and trivia about Japan.

Clearly, I didn't expect to encounter culture shock or experience much change in the year ahead. I was certain that Japan would be exactly as I remembered it. I was confident that a little experience like living abroad for a year would not change me in the least.

After all, thanks to my recent encounter with God—the kinder, gentler, and less demanding God—I was more comfortable being me than I'd ever been before. The last thing I wanted was to be displaced again, literally or figuratively. Life was finally making sense, and I wanted to enjoy this stability for a while.

I must have thought that going to Japan during my third year of college would be like hitting the Pause button on my life. Everything on the screen would freeze while I took off on a fun adventure, and when I hit Play upon my return to the U.S., everything would resume—just as if nothing had happened.

I distinctly recall saying to a friend after my bon voyage party, "I hope I don't change"—and my friend just laughed. How could a person not change after living in another country for a year?

At the time, however, the irony was lost on me. I was going to Japan in order to attend college, not to let the experience change me.

THE FIRST THING I NOTICED AFTER LANDING in Japan was that I was very tired.

We had left Los Angeles midmorning. By the time we finally landed, it was way past midnight California time. I had heard about jet lag, but the farthest distance I ever traveled in the past decade was between New York and California, which is only a three-hour time difference. California to Japan is a sixteen-hour time difference. My day and night were completely flipped, and I didn't like it. If I had experienced the reverse twelve years earlier when we moved from Japan, I was too young and excited to notice.

We students groggily retrieved our luggage and walked out of customs, where we saw an ICU representative holding a welcome sign. She greeted us warmly and helped us board a bus that took us on a two-hour ride through Tokyo traffic to our destination.

During the drive, this representative walked around the bus introducing herself and getting to know each of us. A Canadian ex-pat who had been living in Japan with her husband for over ten years, Mrs. Harder was the coordinator for the exchange program's new arrivals. She probably moved to Japan around the same time I had left. She was gregarious and very talkative, and I appreciated her kind welcome, but I just wanted her to leave me alone and let me sleep. I couldn't believe my bright-eyed fellow riders who were excitedly pointing out every landmark we drove by!

Nothing outside the window looked remotely familiar to me. But then, I remembered, I had grown up in Osaka, not Tokyo. The only time I had been in Tokyo as a little girl was when we were flying out of the country, and even then the airport we flew out of was Haneda, not Narita. That airport was built sometime after we moved to the U.S.

I kept looking out the window for something—anything—recognizable. All I saw were nondescript concrete buildings. Cars looked much smaller than what I was used to. The streets were crowded and the roads much narrower than I recalled from my childhood. We might as well have landed on Mars.

When we finally got off the air-conditioned bus, Mrs. Harder directed us to the on-campus dormitories we would call home for the summer. A stifling humidity overwhelmed me as I pulled my suitcase along the walkway leading up to my dorm. I had noticed the heat and humidity when I was at the airport, but I somehow thought the jets of the planes were causing it there. *Surely it won't be like this when we get to the school,* I had hoped.

Then it dawned on me. This was mid-June. The tsuyu season would start any day now. *This is only the beginning of the monsoonal weather in Japan!*

I had totally forgotten about it. California summers are desert-like ("It's a *dry* heat") and much more tolerable. The only time we Californians experience such humidity is in a sauna, which is fun; this was not.

I have to endure this awful heat and humidity not just for the rest of this afternoon, not only for the rest of this week, but for the next couple months? A raging headache began as sweat dripped down my back. I was tired, hot, and hungry, but mostly I was sleepy. I decided to call it a day and went to get settled in my room.

MY ROOMMATE, LYNN, WAS A FRECKLED strawberry-blonde from UC Davis. Before I could begin to carry on a coherent conversation, however, I needed a shower.

So I went to the shower area and turned on both the red and blue knobs. Only cold water came out. I waited a minute or two for the water to heat up, but it didn't warm up at all. After a few more minutes, I shut off the shower and went to the front desk to report the problem.

I could not believe what they told me: the dorm's water heater was turned on only between six and nine at night. It was five o'clock; if I didn't want to wait, I was stuck with a cold shower.

Running hot water for only three hours a day? Are these people barbaric? My annoyance flared as I did a quick rinse in the icy water and got out as fast as I could.

I returned to my room to lie down, but by the time my head hit the pillow I was sweating. A fan whirred in the corner, but all it did was stir the hot, humid air. Too exhausted to care, I drifted off to sleep, hoping and praying I would wake up from this nightmare.

The sun was rising when I awoke the next morning. My mood had improved, thanks to a good night's rest, and I bounded out of bed to look out the window. *Japan! At last!*

I went to the cafeteria with Lynn as soon as it opened for breakfast. Rice and miso soup for breakfast is the absolute best! I had never seen *that* on a cafeteria menu at UC Irvine.

We Japanese consider rice to be central to our culinary life, almost sacred. In fact, the Japanese word for *rice* is the same as the word for a *meal: gohan*. In Japanese meals, the rice is always considered the main dish and all the other side dishes mere accoutrements, which we call *okazu*. No matter how long I live in America, my tummy and taste buds forever remain Japanese, and nothing satisfies me when I am truly hungry the way rice and a little bit of okazu can. Add a little hot miso soup, and I am immediately transported back to my mom's kitchen in Osaka.

And now I could get that every morning in the school cafeteria? Yum!

At the table, I met students from a few other countries—Hong Kong, Korea, Sweden, France, and Kenya—who were also there for the summer language program. It was like the United Nations. I couldn't help but wonder if these were future leaders of our world. I tried to make note of each name, not only for the short term but also in case I one day read that they had won a Nobel Prize or become the prime minister of their nation.

Some of the students came from countries like Brazil and Korea, where English is not spoken. I felt sorry for them, because ICU students were expected to speak in either Japanese or English. At that time the dominant foreign language in Japan was English, so a person who didn't speak one of those two languages was completely left out.

In a world of only Japanese and English, these highly intelligent young adults were struggling to communicate their breakfast order. It was a stark reminder that people judge each other by the way they speak. No matter how smart or accomplished someone is, their IQ is gauged by their grasp on language. Life just isn't fair.

AFTER BREAKFAST, ALL OF US STUDENTS WENT to yet another orientation, where this time we heard speeches by university dignitaries. We sang a hymn in both English and Japanese accompanied by an impressive pipe organ that shook the walls of the campus chapel.

Then we were sent to our respective classrooms. I walked past the classrooms for Levels 1, 2, and 3 without even glancing at the lists of names. Outside the Advanced 1 classroom, I slowed down to check the posted list. My name was not on it.

I went to the Advanced 2 list. *Hmmm, not there either.*

I was ready to go talk to the language department staff about their mistake when I noticed a room with the sign Special Japanese posted outside.

Special sounded like a euphemism for *remedial*. Curious to see what poor souls were so lacking in language skills that they would be assigned to this group, I walked over to check out the list.

There was my name.

I couldn't believe my eyes. *I am a* remedial *student? But Japanese is my mother tongue!*

Reluctantly, I walked inside and took a seat. But I didn't place my bag on the floor; I kept it on my lap. I was not ready to commit myself to the classroom. Yet.

There were eight students besides me, and from the looks of it, I was not the only one in shock.

The teacher greeted us and asked us to introduce ourselves. As I listened to each story, I realized that they were a lot like me. We had all grown up abroad in Japanese-speaking homes, so our spoken language skills were pretty good. However, we didn't know much grammar, we lacked a wide vocabulary, and most of us were at a third-grade level for reading and a first-grade level for writing. Most of the blond folks in the other classrooms, students barely able to converse with store clerks, could run circles around us when it came to *kanji* writing skills.

Besides not having taken any college-level courses in Japanese, most of us in this class also had spotty attendance records at Saturday

Japanese schools. After we reviewed our scores from the Japanese test we had taken before departure, there was no denying that we needed this...uh...special class.

We were humbled. And we knew we were in for a long, arduous summer.

SOME FOUR-YEAR ICU STUDENTS HAD stayed on campus to work during the summer. Most were Japanese nationals who wanted to interact with international students in order to polish their English skills. Others were foreign exchange students who couldn't afford to fly home for the summer and chose to stay in the dorms. Some of them volunteered or worked with the summer language program, some served in the cafeteria, and some just hung out and occasionally took off to hitchhike around Japan.

I tried to befriend Japanese students who were about my age, but I was surprised by my lack of conversational skills. I could only talk about trivial things on a superficial level because there weren't enough entries in my internal third-grade-level dictionary to express myself.

Trying to converse in Japanese was tiring work, so I soon found myself gravitating toward students from the States. This made me feel guilty; I should be reaching out and utilizing this wonderful cultural exchange opportunity. I worried that I was wasting my parents' hard-earned money, but I was having a hard enough time just surviving!

I also discovered that these Japanese girls were different from the last Japanese friends I'd had, in New York. When I was nine or ten, friendship was easy: I could strike up a conversation with anyone and everyone, and we just played. We flew kites, had fun on the playground, and looked for marine animals and mythical figures in the clouds. We certainly didn't go to nightclubs or sit at local coffee houses discussing politics and philosophy, which these college students liked to do...for hours.

According to my parents while growing up, Japanese girls got perfect grades, studied hard, never talked back, and were sweet little angels. The girls I met at the university, however, were not so angelic. Some of them even smoked! They all seemed so grown up and worldly, not at all what I imagined.

After the six-week language course ended, I had some time to travel around Japan before the fall semester started. So I went back to Fujiidera, the city I lived in before moving to the States.

My heart pounded with excitement as I walked from the train station toward the house we'd called home. It was still there, aluminum shutters and all. The backyard looked the same, sans the dog. I was sad to see that nearly all the rice paddies around our house had disappeared. Everywhere I looked, new homes had replaced the dirt paths I used to run along while flying my kite.

I thrilled to hear the familiar sounds of cicadas buzzing and frogs croaking in the summer heat. It was just as I remembered from my childhood.

That's when I noticed something surprising. The house had shrunk! I could have sworn it was so much bigger. Maybe it shrank in the heat each summer, I thought, like wool sweaters do when laundered in hot water.

I was also shocked to see that the highway running in front of our house was now a quiet two-lane road. I always thought we lived on a major thoroughfare. I could still hear the huge cars and monster trucks that rumbled by. When I crossed the street at the corner signal, I had to toddle with all my might to make it before the light turned red.

Why is everything so much smaller?

Then it dawned on me. I was looking at exactly the same house on exactly the same road. I had grown bigger!

IN THE ALMOST TWO MONTHS SINCE I arrived in Japan, my list of disappointments had multiplied. This was not the "homecoming" I had imagined.

I didn't fit in anywhere. Not here in Japan, and certainly not in America. For the first time, I wasn't really sure if I was Japanese or American.

Who am I? I want to go home, but where is my home?

Then one day a verse in Ephesians caught my attention:

Consequently, you are no longer foreigners and aliens, but fellow citizens with God's people and members of God's household. (Ephesians 2:19)

Foreigners and aliens. That sounded like me! I actually had dual citizenship, but I felt like I didn't belong anywhere.

I was born in New York, where my parents lived while my father was on his first work assignment—just long enough for my sister and me to get our U.S. citizenships. Then we moved back to Japan. I got my Japanese citizenship based on the fact that I am of Japanese ancestry, and my parents registered my birth at the city hall upon their return.

When we returned to New York in 1969, I used my newly issued Japanese passport. When I came back to Japan this time, I used my newly issued U.S. passport. On both occasions I entered the country as a foreigner. *It's like I don't have a homeland anymore! Wherever I go, I'm a foreigner.*

But the verse in Ephesians suddenly made clear that I do have a homeland—in heaven.

I am a fellow citizen with God's people. It doesn't matter where my citizenship lies, because my true citizenship is in heaven with God. My homeland is not Japan, the U.S., or anywhere on earth. My true homeland is somewhere I haven't been to yet, but someday I will spend an eternity there with Jesus.

That is my true homeland. I came from the Land of the Rising Sun; now my true citizenship is in the land of the risen Son!

THE REGULAR SCHOOL YEAR BEGAN in earnest that fall. To my surprise, I began to enjoy not only my time at ICU but also life in general. I started to notice the world beyond myself. I discovered some fascinating people.

I made friends from countries around the world. I even tried foods from other countries. What a difference it made, to know who I was! My identity lay in Jesus and his redemptive love for me; this allowed me to reach out to others and truly enjoy their company.

Too often these days we say to one another, "Celebrate diversity!" and "Accept others just the way they are!" without even knowing who we ourselves are. Outwardly, we may look as if we're celebrating diversity, but inwardly we are jealously guarding who we think we ought to be and judging others because of their differences.

But how can we accept other people when we can't even accept ourselves? It is only when we find security in the living God that we truly and wholeheartedly accept others...as well as ourselves.

God had taught me much in the past year. At UCI, I learned that his perfection covers me and that I no longer have to strive to achieve perfection in my own power. In Japan, God taught me that my citizenship is in heaven and my identity in him. I wondered, *What will you teach me next, Lord?*

I never could have imagined the surprise God had in store for me.

7

My Superstar Friend
Junko

"Vanity of vanities!
All is vanity."
ECCLESIASTES 1:2, NASB

One Sunday morning just before I left the States for my year in Japan, I sat next to a nice woman at church. After the hymn our pastor had us turn to our neighbors and greet them, so I turned to say hello.

The woman's name was Mrs. Melilli, and I learned that her daughter and I had sung together in high school choir. I also found out that Mrs. Melilli had recently hosted a young Japanese woman named Junko. She was a singer in Japan who had just released her debut album, and she had visited the U.S. on a home stay to improve her English. While she was staying with the Melillis, Junko received a call from her record company in Tokyo: her single had gone to number one on the hit charts. It would be the first of many.

When Mrs. Melilli learned that I was going to Japan, she insisted on giving me Junko's number. I was completely out of touch with the Japanese pop (J-pop) music scene at that time, so I had no idea who was popular in Japan. I certainly didn't know who Junko was or what she sounded like.

That didn't keep me from making the call, though. I used the pay phone in the dorms. Junko, delighted to hear from someone personally sent by Mrs. Melilli, immediately made plans for us to get together.

Since I made the call within a week or two of my arrival, my Japanese was so awkward that I almost couldn't explain how I had gotten Junko's number. Fortunately, her English was quite good—thanks in part to the two weeks she spent in the U.S.—so she switched to English without skipping a beat. She seemed pleased to be able to speak to a native English speaker, which I suppose I had become.

When I asked the Japanese girls around ICU if they had ever heard of this Junko, they all seemed to know her. When I told them I was getting together with her in a few days, they were flabbergasted. It was akin to my telling someone today that I was meeting Lady Gaga or Britney Spears for coffee. People would think I was either lying or out of my mind...which is probably what my ICU friends thought, too.

JUNKO ASKED ME TO MEET HER IN the middle of Tokyo, at a famous dog statue outside the Shibuya train station. It was noon on a humid summer day. About fifteen minutes after our appointed meet time, she drove up in an American car. Only a few years older than me, yet she already owned a car—a major luxury for most Japanese!

Junko spotted me and waved me over. Although I didn't know exactly what she looked like, right away I knew this was Junko: in Japan, cars drive on the left side of the road. Junko's foreign car, with the steering wheel on the "wrong" side, really stood out.

As I jumped into the car, she apologized profusely for being late. Her TV appearance had taken much longer than expected.

Right away she asked me all about Mrs. Melilli and her family. Unfortunately, I didn't have a lot of information to share—we'd only had a two-minute conversation during the greeting time at church and a few more minutes after the service to exchange phone numbers.

Junko asked what I like to eat for lunch. When I told her cold soba (buckwheat noodles, a popular summer dish when served cold), she responded that it was also her favorite. We headed to her favorite soba place.

As soon as we stepped into the restaurant, all eyes were on us. People were whispering and pointing, and I am pretty sure they weren't pointing at me.

Junko ignored the commotion and, after getting us the best table in the house, started ordering the best soba in town. She told me about the fun she'd had during the two weeks she spent in the States, and she reminisced about the fabulous places she visited. She had definitely seen much more of the U.S. than I had.

She was, in a curious way, more American than I was.

Our next stop was a Yamaha music store to pick up the latest model of her favorite keyboard. When we stepped into the store, once again the staring and whispering started. She sat down at the keyboard to test it out and played a few bars of one of her songs, the one which evidently was her current number one hit. People began crowding around as if it were an impromptu concert. Again, their gazes went right to Junko. I felt invisible, but also proud. I still hadn't heard any of her music but could tell by the crowd's reaction that Junko's music touched many hearts.

After that we were off to a high-end boutique in the fashion district of Tokyo, to look for clothes for Junko's next TV appearance. The designer and her staff served us bottomless tea and coffee while bringing out racks and racks of clothes from the latest collection. As Junko tried on different outfits, the entire store *oohed* and *aahed*. Meanwhile, I just kept running to the restroom after drinking all that tea and coffee.

Junko was kind enough to introduce me to each person in the store, and they all agreed that I looked very American and that I was so tanned and slim. Then the conversation immediately turned back to the star.

Perched decoratively next to her, I felt a little like a teacup chihuahua. But Junko seemed pleased to have me, an American friend, near her. And I was proud to be hanging out with a famous person. This was definitely a win-win.

Finally, feeling we had been out enough that day, Junko announced that we would eat in for dinner. We went to a grocery store to buy ingredients for the meal, and it wasn't long before people started noticing her again. The man at the register quaked with excitement as he rang us up. A few people asked Junko to autograph the backs of their receipts.

Junko's new apartment was located in a very expensive section of Tokyo. She wasn't completely unpacked and her furniture hadn't arrived yet, so we improvised. We ate our chicken dinner on the floor using a cardboard box as a table, with a bedsheet draped over the top. We laughed throughout the meal.

In the privacy of her own home, Junko relaxed. Her smile was more genuine than the professional smile she wore around town. I could tell she was happy to be with someone who didn't want to be with her just because of her fame.

After our fun day together, she drove me to a train station, where

I took a quick ride back to ICU. As soon as I walked into the dorms, the Japanese girls gathered around me. *What's she like? What did you do? How tall is she? Is she nice?*

I shared details about what we did, what we ate, and where we went. And I told them that Junko is quite short (several inches shorter than me!) and really nice. Then they ran to the phones to tell their friends and family about my day with Junko. I couldn't believe all the fuss!

I got to spend only a couple more days with Junko the rest of the year. Her life got increasingly busier with each successive hit. No longer did anyone have to be a J-pop expert to know about this girl. She was everywhere—TV, radio, billboards, commercials, and magazine covers. You couldn't *not* hear her or see her.

Whenever I saw Junko on TV, I understood why my friends were so surprised to learn that she was tiny in person. She looked so tall onscreen! Her powerful, velvety voice equally betrayed her small stature. In fact, everything about her seemed larger than life.

This very famous person—who coincidentally shared my name—defined fame. And I had gotten an insider's view of her life.

𝒥 MUST CONFESS, I GREW UP HOPING TO one day be famous myself. Maybe many young girls feel that way—I know my preteen daughter and most of her friends do!

As a seven-year-old in Osaka, I couldn't wait to sing on TV. I wanted a radio hit that would let the world know I had arrived. I pictured myself surrounded by adoring fans, and I vowed to be a positive influence on my very impressionable young admirers. I also promised myself that I would never let fame change me, and that I would use my notoriety to further charitable causes.

After spending time with Junko, however, I realized that fame definitely has its downside. For example, the utter lack of privacy.

Junko was truly talented. Her songs, which she wrote herself, were quite good, and her voice very pleasant. Rather than being gossip-magazine fodder, she was actually popular for her talents. (We can all think of talentless "stars" who are famous merely for being famous. Their images are splashed all over the Internet and the covers of celebrity magazines, and they eventually come out with their own line of clothing before disappearing altogether.)

Junko was probably only a year or two into her most famous years when I spent time with her, but she seemed already to have tired of the attention. She was more interested in making music; her fame was merely a vehicle.

Sure, she had to sell her persona and make appearances here and there, and she seemed able to play that game to her advantage. It was all a part of the gig. She had learned to accept it and juggle its demands well.

As I mentioned earlier, ICU had its share of celebrities—something I eventually figured out.

When I arrived, I was as unaware of the Japanese movie scene as I was of pop music. But evidently, a few famous actors and actresses were enrolled at ICU with me. I say *enrolled* because we never saw them actually attend class. They were ICU students in name only. Busy filming schedules kept them away quite often. How they graduated is a mystery to me, but I didn't ask questions.

Several other students and some professors appeared regularly not in movies, but on an educational show on the government-subsidized TV station NHK. The Japanese have always been eager to learn English, and NHK offered English conversation lessons via radio and television.

The shows were called *Eigo Kaiwa* (*"English Conversation"*) *I, II, and III.* The Level I show was the most entertaining and therefore most watched; on the air four times a week, this program regularly had a viewership of two to three million people. (My hunch, though, is that most Japanese left *Eigo Kaiwa* on in the background while they did household chores, hoping they would somehow learn English by osmosis.)

One of the Japanese professors who taught English at ICU was a regular instructor on this TV show, and he often recruited English-speaking exchange students to appear as actors in the vignettes. Most of these students were not actors, but the fact that they were native English speakers trumped their lack of acting skills. This meant that the better actors were asked back for repeat performances.

One such standout was a Japanese American named Kenny, a recent UCLA graduate who came to ICU for the language course. After the summer ended, Kenny decided to stay in Japan to get to know his roots and teach English privately. Having taken some theater courses while at UCLA, he was actually a decent actor. The professor at ICU championed Kenny for a regular role on *Eigo Kaiwa I.* With his Jackie Chan–like good looks, Kenny soon had many young ladies watching the show and boosting the program's ratings.

This Level I English conversation series also featured a music segment called "Song Album" halfway through each thirty-minute program. They usually had a singer or a band perform an American Top 40 hit while they superimposed the English lyrics on the screen so that listeners could work on understanding spoken English.

No matter how good the Japanese singers were, their English was always affected by their accents. This fact left the producer scrambling for other singers. What the show really needed was someone who spoke English like a native and could also sing—at the time, a rare find in Japan.

At some point during the summer language intensive program, Kenny and I realized that he played the guitar and I sang, so we put together an act and called ourselves Kenny & Junko. We made a few appearances at the campus talent shows and at the ICU cafe's open mike nights. The producer of *Eigo Kaiwa I* got wind of us from the ICU professor and called us in for an audition. Mr. Kojima liked us and immediately asked us to perform on the show.

Are you kidding? Me? Sing on national television? I thought I would float off the ground in excitement! When they offered to pay us each 10,000 yen (equivalent to about $100 today) per song, plus the cost of the taxi ride back to the campus afterward, that sealed the deal.

Wow, I'm going to be a professional singer! I'm going to be famous! This, I thought, was truly my dream come true.

BETWEEN MY CLASSES, KENNY AND I practiced three songs—a Beatles tune, a Carpenters hit, and a ballad by Olivia Newton-John. And a few weeks later, we showed up for our very first TV shoot.

We walked into the big lobby of the sprawling NHK complex in Shibuya and signed the visitor log. I recognized the names of a few famous Japanese also visiting the studios that day.

Mr. Kojima's assistant met us and took us through a maze of halls to our studio and dressing rooms. As I sat on the chair having my makeup done in front of bright lights, I thought, *I have truly arrived. This must be what Junko experiences every single day!*

When we walked into the studio, the set was arranged. Two

cameras had been put in place just for me—and Kenny, too, of course. Then the crew counted down, the cameras started rolling, Kenny began to play his guitar, and I started singing the songs I knew so well.

By God's grace, I nailed it. Mr. Kojima decided to do a second take, just for backup; but I could tell he already had more than enough to work with.

I was almost as relieved as the producer and crew were: I hadn't disappointed them! After all, they were investing in an unknown college student with little experience beyond church solos and high school choir ensembles.

It would be about another month before the first footage of Kenny & Junko actually aired on *Eigo Kaiwa I*. The moment I heard from Kenny the date of our big debut, I called all of my relatives and friends around the country to make sure they tuned in.

There was one TV in the common area of our dorm, and I gathered as many friends as I could—five or six—to watch with me. My dorm mates had watched other friends appear on the show as actors from time to time, but this was the first time a fellow student was going to be a vocalist on the show.

When I came onscreen, they all clapped. During the song, they patted me on the back. When it was over, they applauded. I reveled in the attention.

Then, seemingly within seconds, they returned to whatever they had been doing before the show began—homework, studying, hanging out with friends.

Is this it? Where did everyone go? Having very much enjoyed their attention, I marveled at how fleeting was that moment of glory. I turned off the TV and returned to my room to finish my own homework. Deadlines had to be met.

I decided to perform an experiment when Kenny and I appeared on the show a couple of weeks later. There was a lounge at ICU where students hung out in the afternoons before the cafeteria opened for dinner. The TV in that lounge was always on, mounted high in the corner for everyone to watch, and it was almost always turned to the NHK channel.

Kenny and I decided to sit near that TV when our second appearance aired. We wanted to see if anyone noticed that we were on television.

When my onscreen self began to sing, a few people looked up from their homework or conversation to comment—"Oh, I've always liked this Beatles song"—but nobody realized that *I* was the one on the screen.

Even when I walked up to the TV, stood right next to the screen, and faced the people in the lounge, no one noticed. A friend walked into the room and waved at me, but after a brief glance at the TV, she made a beeline to the vending machine.

She hadn't even noticed that I was the person singing on the show. *People, do you not realize that you are one of two or three million people watching me at this very moment? Your star is right in front of you!*

The room was abuzz with conversations, and they weren't about me. Kenny was just as amazed as I was by people's oblivion, although he was probably more amused by the whole thing. I felt very disappointed.

I LEARNED FROM MY STUDENT LOUNGE experiment how fleeting fame is. Granted, I didn't hit the J-pop scene full force as my friend Junko had, but I realized that most people are too busy with their own lives to care—to truly care—about a famous person.

Oh, they might claim to be a fan of this band or that singer, but most people don't really care about the celebrity's well-being. Even Junko's fans, after snapping photos with her or getting an autograph, after experiencing the thrill of meeting her, went back to minding their own business. Every single one.

Sure, certain individuals live vicariously through famous people and hang out all day with their posse of groupies (don't they have jobs or go to school?). But it seems empty to get one's self-worth simply from associating with someone famous.

I enjoyed hanging out with Junko and receiving some of her fans' attention, but I knew they were only interested in me to the extent that I was an extension of the real attraction. I wanted Junko's fans to get to know me *because*, I was screaming on the inside that day we hung out, *I am an interesting person in my own right!*

Even when I was the TV "star," the thrill of being the center of attention lasted only a few moments. I realized that I would much rather enjoy deeper friendships with people who like me for being me rather than for being famous.

Granted, I never reached the fame status of a big-time celebrity. But I got enough of a taste of it—from my day with Junko as well as my appearances on *Eigo Kaiwa I*—to know that one ought not build a life upon such shaky ground.

Besides, it is amazing how fickle the public is. A person can become a huge star overnight but within a few weeks be completely forgotten. In the short year I lived in Japan, for instance, I noticed quite a turnover in the Top 10 list, although Junko managed to remain there for quite a while.

*B*EFORE LEAVING JAPAN TO FINISH MY degree at UC Irvine, I went on to record a couple more dozen songs for NHK. For most of the '80s, I was on TV in Japan up to four times a week, reportedly watched by millions of viewers a week.

I received some fan letters, mostly from preschool kids who watched the show with their moms during the day.

Even back in Southern California shopping malls, I was occasionally recognized by Japanese tourists who had probably diligently watched *Eigo Kaiwa I* before their big trip to America. The whole experience made my parents and relatives very proud, and for that I am forever grateful for my NHK experience.

Even now, from time to time I occasionally run into Japanese folks who remember me from the show. One mom in particular recognized me because she regularly watched *Eigo Kaiwa I* with her dad while she was a high school student in Japan. She had married an American, and her kids now attend the same school as my kids do.

One day she asked me for a photograph to send to her father back home. I gladly obliged. Afterward there was an awkward silence, followed by chitchat about our kids' homework and the upcoming book fair. Good thing my whole identity isn't based on my past glory days on NHK television!

In 2010, video clips of Kenny & Junko appearances submitted by unknown fans began popping up on YouTube. This many years later, I am able to watch my performances more objectively. I cringe to see my earnest but very nervous twenty-year-old self onstage. Mind you, I got through without any mistakes, but that's the best I can say about my performance!

Oh, and if you think I made it rich with my TV appearances? I didn't receive a yen beyond what I got paid the day I actually sang in front of the camera. We musicians had best keep our day jobs.

𝒟URING ONE NHK TAPING, A GROUP OF KIDS from the local elementary school stopped by on a field trip and stayed to watch us rehearse a song. They all shook hands with Kenny and me afterward, and some of the teachers asked for my autograph.

I wanted to tell them that I'm really a nobody, but instead I just smiled and obliged. I could tell from the gleam in some of the second-grade girls' eyes that they were thinking the same things I had been at their age: *I am going to be a star one day!*

There's nothing wrong with having a goal to work toward, but I wish I could have told them what I've since learned. It is stated best in the book of Ecclesiastes:

> *Smoke, nothing but smoke. [That's what the Quester says.]*
> *There's nothing to anything—it's all smoke.*
> *What's there to show for a lifetime of work,*
> *a lifetime of working your fingers to the bone?*
> *One generation goes its way, the next one arrives,*
> *but nothing changes—it's business as usual for old planet*
> *earth…*
> *Does someone call out, "Hey, this is new"?*
> *Don't get excited—it's the same old story.*
> *Nobody remembers what happened yesterday.*
> *And the things that will happen tomorrow?*
> *Nobody'll remember them either.*
> *Don't count on being remembered.*
> (Ecclesiastes 1:2–4, 10–11, The Message)

However, I kept quiet. The benefit of hindsight has revealed that some lessons can only be learned, not taught. Yes, it's great to set goals and accomplish them. But don't count on being remembered, even tomorrow.

8

SIMMERING ON THE BACK BURNER

All things are lawful,
but not all things edify.
1 CORINTHIANS 10:23, NASB

I really enjoy life and like to live each day to the fullest. For some people, that might mean partying the night away. Others skydive, snorkel, tackle any other outdoor adventure they can find.

In my early twenties, "living life to the fullest" meant…predict-ability. Now, I know that is not exactly awe-inspiring. But it is the truth.

I wanted to make sure I had a steady paycheck showing up every other week that would cover my rent and car payments. I also wanted to run or get some sort of exercise pretty much every day, to sing in the choir at church, and to attend the worship service every Sunday.

I liked my routine. And I must have seemed like an old lady.

This is all quite ironic, because today I'm much more adventurous than I ever was in my not-at-all-wild, very predictable twenties. And now I actually *am* an old lady! (Okay, not really. But I'm on my way there.)

My need for predictability meant one thing: no matter how much I enjoyed making music, I wasn't willing to be a starving musician. I could have stayed in Japan indefinitely, singing more songs on NHK and possibly expanding my musical horizons there. But instead I returned to UC Irvine to finish my college education. I wanted a degree.

My choice of major—computer science—was a gamble that paid off. After graduation, I found a job as a programmer fairly quickly while my friends with other majors had a tougher go. I received a decent salary, had an apartment with a couple of Christian gals, and lived the nine-to-five drill of a young professional.

Soon I discovered that after working all day—because each workday lasted much longer than eight hours, especially with commuting time factored in—I could fit in only one other activity after work. If I grabbed dinner with a friend, it meant my running was out for that day, which would necessitate doubling my distance the next day. Weekends were spent catching up on office work, doing laundry, and grocery shopping. Sundays I attended church and got together with my parents for dinner.

And then the week started all over again.

I USED TO THINK THAT YOUNG professionals who dressed in business attire, flew around the country on business trips, and drove fast cars led such glamorous lives. However, it wasn't long before I started to see this routine as a real grind.

Long hours in the office forced me to put my dreams on hold.

I could still hear Rich Briggs's words: "Are you doing something each and every day that moves you closer to your goal?" Even with that question echoing in my mind, day after day went by without my doing much more than surviving.

Sure, I enjoyed the company of my colleagues and was making a decent living. But I knew in my heart that this life was fueled by neither passion nor a response to my calling.

My passion was music. I wanted to write songs, and I wanted to perform them. Writing code for mainframe computers just was so…dry.

After a time, I was given the opportunity to make technical presentations for marketing people. That additional responsibility made the job a little more interesting. Still, I knew this work was not my calling.

Contributing to that knowledge was a lesson I learned very quickly: unlike some of the tech geniuses within the company, I was just average. Truly brilliant programmers literally lost track of time and stayed in their cubicles all night long writing code. After pulling all-nighters, their faces glowed green from staring at their computer screen for hours. They smelled like they hadn't showered in days. Writing code was their passion.

I liked my life—and valued my personal hygiene—far too much to try or even want to be like them.

Whatever I do, though, I put everything into it. So it wasn't long before I worked my way up the corporate ladder. The result was that I got caught up in the moment—a moment that lasted many years.

Never did I pause to evaluate whether I was doing what I should be doing. Was I in God's will? Was I fully living the kind of life he had planned for me?

God created every human being to serve him. For each individual, that avenue of service will in some way be unique. Many believers find their calling in a corporation and do as unto the Lord their absolute best in their profession.

However, I felt a restlessness every day. That restlessness, I see now, should have been a clue that I wasn't doing all I was supposed to be doing.

ABOUT FIVE YEARS INTO MY CAREER AT Unisys Corporation, the marketing department at the headquarters in Detroit launched a new product and was searching for a jingle to go along with their marketing campaign. When they heard through the corporate grapevine that I was a musician, they gave me a call. I was commissioned to write the jingle! Through my voice teacher at the time, I was introduced to someone who could help produce the ditty I came up with: a drummer and producer named Dave Spurr. He had been touring with the Maranatha! Singers with his wife, Cathy, who is also a musician. She, along with her friend Debbie McNeil, were signed to Maranatha! Records as the duo Spurr & McNeil. I had heard some of their beautiful songs on the Christian radio many times.

Dave came up with a wonderful instrumental track for my jingle, and I recorded the vocals in Dave and Cathy's small studio at their house. Their recording setup was modest, as was their home in Moreno Valley, California, but I felt as though I were recording at Capitol Records in Hollywood. It was my first professional recording of my own composition—albeit just thirty seconds long. Best of all, the marketing people loved it! I was able to take part in the big unveiling of the new product line a few weeks later and got a taste of a life much more exciting than your typical cubicle-abiding programmer.

The marketing group subsequently asked me to write a few more jingles, and I became somewhat of an in-house corporate jingle writer for Unisys.

What I recall about that experience is how much fun I had working on that little tune. I felt so *alive*. I also got a glimpse into the lives of some full-time musicians. Sure, Dave and Cathy led modest lives, but their hearts were filled with passion. Debbie and Cathy were very disciplined about songwriting, meeting weekly to write song after song, and they made a decent living from song royalties. Most of all, they trusted that the Lord would provide for their income and their lives. They lived their lives dangerously—much more so than I ever did at that point in my life.

After a while, I realized that I was not fully trusting the Lord with my life. I was choosing the material comforts my job provided over trusting that God would provide if I used the gifts he gave me. I knew I was settling for something less.

NOW, LET ME CLARIFY: I'M NOT SAYING that everyone needs to shirk life's responsibilities and pursue their passion. In my case, though, I needed to either fully pursue my calling or let go of my dream of music. I was tired of asking myself, "What if...?" and not taking action.

Some people have a passion outside of their work but maintain that passion as a hobby and are perfectly fine that way. For instance, I have a couple of friends who are wonderful musicians—Kevin on guitar and Marty on piano. Either of those talented men could probably earn a decent living doing studio work or playing around town.

But they choose to do music on the weekends at clubs or church, for the pure enjoyment of it. They enjoy these weekend opportunities to showcase their musical talents, and they do not worry about money because they make their living doing something else. After all, being a professional musician isn't easy.

It's just that my work as a computer programmer was all-consuming. My dream had been left on the back burner. I struggled and lived with this inner turmoil for seven years after graduating from college. I had to make a decision.

From where I stand now, I don't regret the years I spent in the corporate world. For one thing, I was able to save the money I needed to make my first CD. In that sense, I did something every day to reach my ultimate goal: earn enough money to eventually become a full-time musician. In time I became a computer consultant, at which point I enjoyed an hourly income and a more flexible schedule.

But it took several years. And sometimes I wonder if I might have taken a less circuitous route. For example, I could have scaled back my lifestyle—driven a less expensive car or lived in a less expensive neighborhood. I might have saved up enough money to make my demo recording or attend a songwriter's conference sooner. I could have worked in a less demanding profession or cut back my hours to have the energy to write more music.

I don't think too hard about this, though. God has redeemed that time and made something beautiful out of my life. For that truth, for that promise fulfilled, I am grateful.

MY YEARS IN THE CORPORATE WORLD yielded at least one positive: my ability to relate to audience members who are corporate professionals. A majority of the people I sing for are, in fact, in engineering or computer-related fields. (Yes, I sing at a lot of Asian churches!)

Having worked a similar vocation, I have a good sense of what the folks in my audience go through each day. I know what it means to show up for work early, to meet deadlines and finish projects according to specs and a client's timeline, and to work with…uh… "challenging" people as part of a team. I know how it feels to go through an annual review. I understand the politics of the corporate world. I have lived that life myself.

Not until I met David, my soul mate and husband of more than two decades, did I find the courage to step out in faith and make music my career. David is my safe haven, with whom I share all my dreams. He validates my fears yet encourages my passion. With his support, I can pursue my calling with full abandon.

When we first met, David and I were both recent college grads.

But I knew *of* him long before that. My sister Reiko, who attended the University of California in San Diego (UCSD), kept telling me about a guy named David Cheng. "He often says the same thing as you do and looks at life just like you, Junko," she enthused. "Sometimes when he's speaking to me, I feel like you're the one speaking!"

She kept talking about David for a couple of years, but I assumed—based on the description Reiko gave of a smart Chinese American, serious, strong Christian, and total "study animal"—that he must look like a nerd.

Upon graduation from UCSD, David got accepted to the medical school at UC Irvine and moved into the apartment on campus about the same time I graduated from UCI and began my professional life nearby. Reiko had given him my phone number, and although we chatted a few times, my assumptions about this intelligent Asian guy kept me from making any plans to get together.

Imagine my surprise when, one day, he showed up at my church in Irvine. He was kind of cute! I especially liked his eyes. I enjoyed talking with him and could tell right away that he would be a great buddy...but no more. He just didn't fit my mental picture of someone I would date or even consider marrying.

At the time, I was fully convinced I was going to marry a guy with blue eyes and blond hair. You see, if I wasn't ever going to become a Caucasian, I was at least going to marry one and get myself an Anglo last name! At least, that was my line of logic. (Yeah, I know, I'm a bit embarrassed and ashamed at such shallow thinking, but at the time it made sense.)

However, our phone conversations became more frequent and deeper as the months went on. We told each other our life goals, hopes, and dreams. David believed in mine, and I believed in his. I really enjoyed his company.

One day about a year into our friendship, I was mentally going down the list of the great qualities I saw in David. Christian—check. Smart—check. Responsible—yes. Athletic—sure. Good conversationalist—yup. Makes me laugh—yes! And on it went, until it began to dawn on me that those were all the qualities I had been seeking in the Ideal Man all along.

The only discrepancy was his ethnicity, but then I realized it was the same as mine! How wrong could that be? The scales fell off my eyes once again, and I began to see David with a lot more appreciation. Slowly, our friendship developed into love, and we finally exchanged our vows in the spring of 1988. (David later told me that *he* had been after me since the day we met. Needless to say, he is a patient but very determined guy!)

GOD PUT MY HUSBAND INTO MY LIFE for many good reasons, and one of them is so I would finally pursue my calling in music. David continues to give me his full support, and I thank the Lord for bringing me such a perfect match for a mate.

After all, until I married David, I really wasn't doing much to develop my songwriting or singing skills. Sure, I sang an occasional solo at church and was part of the church choir. But I wanted music to be a bigger part of my life.

I wasn't all that passionate about jazz, classical, choral, opera, or even music education. But I'd heard about CCM (contemporary Christian music), and that's the genre I wanted to pursue. CCM is basically pop music for the church. I felt that, with the talent and desire God gave me, I would fit best in that arena. I just didn't know *how* to make contemporary Christian music a career.

Then God helped me read the following parable in a new way:

> [The man] called his servants together and delegated responsibilities. To one he gave five thousand dollars, to another two thousand, to a third one thousand, depending on their abilities. Then he left. Right off, the first servant went to work and doubled his master's investment. The second did the same. But the man with the single thousand dug a hole and carefully buried his master's money.
>
> After a long absence, the master of those three servants came back and settled up with them. The one given five thousand dollars showed him how he had doubled his

investment. His master commended him: "Good work! You did your job well. From now on be my partner."

The servant with the two thousand showed how he also had doubled his master's investment. His master commended him: "Good work! You did your job well. From now on be my partner."

The servant given one thousand said, "Master, I know you have high standards and hate careless ways, that you demand the best and make no allowances for error. I was afraid I might disappoint you, so I found a good hiding place and secured your money. Here it is, safe and sound down to the last cent."

The master was furious. "That's a terrible way to live! It's criminal to live cautiously like that! If you knew I was after the best, why did you do less than the least? The least you could have done would have been to invest the sum with the bankers, where at least I would have gotten a little interest.

"Take the thousand and give it to the one who risked the most. And get rid of this 'play-it-safe' who won't go out on a limb. Throw him out into utter darkness." (Matthew 25:14–30, *The Message*)

Throw out into the darkness the servant who had hidden the one thousand? His was a criminal way to live? Wow, that seemed harsh. The servant was merely trying to do what he thought was in the master's best interest...wasn't he?

Maybe it was just an excuse, I rationalized. *Maybe he really was lazy and had wasted his master's talent. Maybe fear paralyzed him and kept him from taking a risk. Perhaps he didn't want to risk losing face if he failed.*

As thoughts like these filled my mind, I found that I couldn't disagree with the master. Even if that servant hadn't received a 200 percent return on an investment in the stock market or some multilevel marketing scheme, he could have at least put the money in the bank to earn a bit of interest.

So, I wondered, *have I buried my talent in the ground?* Perhaps God was calling me to something else, something beyond singing in the church choir. Was the best use of my time and talents working hard at my computer job and singing in the choir on Thursday nights and Sunday mornings?

The choir had been a great avenue to finding my place at a new church. The director's instructions had sharpened me vocally and musically. I also liked using my gifts to serve and build up the fellowship of believers there.

But after eight years, I was at a crossroads: I needed to decide where to invest my musical energy. Sure, the choir took only two hours of my time each Thursday night and another couple of hours on Sunday morning—when I would be at church anyway. Then again, I could have spent those hours writing songs, working on my performing skills, improving my singing, and making contacts so I could sing at other churches and events.

The more I thought about it, the more clearly I saw that singing in the choir was my attempt to "do music" without having to work at it. I wasn't taking risks; I wasn't trusting God's call on my life.

And if I wasn't being obedient to those things, then I was actually (gulp!) sinning.

IT'S IMPORTANT TO TAKE STOCK EVERY ONCE in a while to determine whether our time is being used fruitfully.

Maybe we are called to do something only for a certain season; then we need to change our course. If, after careful and prayerful evaluation, we decide that a particular activity is good and appropriate, then by all means we ought to continue it with energy and joy.

However, if the time for that commitment has passed or if that activity wasn't right in the first place, we need to find the courage to stop and do something else. Before making any rash decisions, though, it is wise to both seek godly counsel and spend time in God's Word. This will help ensure that we are being sensitive and obedient to his direction.

We were created to use our talents for God's glory. He allows us great freedom in how we spend our time, gifting, and money, but we must keep in mind this scriptural truth: "All things are lawful, but not all things are profitable. All things are lawful, but not all things edify" (1 Corinthians 10:23, NASB). I was certainly convicted by that verse.

THERE IS ONE MORE ASPECT OF THIS whole "don't bury your talent" thing that proved a sticking point for me.

In Japanese culture, a person never calls attention to self. My culture teaches that a nail sticking out must be pounded down until it is no longer visible. Conformity is highly esteemed in Japanese society. The logic goes: if you are truly good at something, then others will compliment and elevate you; but don't trumpet your own talents or accomplishments.

Even though I had been an American for a long time, I had—and still have—some very Japanese sides to me. This idea had been so ingrained in me that it was difficult to change.

Who am I, to claim to be a good musician? How presumptuous of me to assume that I have any talent worthy of attention, much less the spotlight! If I'm really good, then managers and agents should be clamoring at my door to guide me to professional success.

So I waited…and waited…and waited…

I was hardly living life to the fullest. Instead, I was biding my time in my little corner of the world, all the while desperately hoping that someone in the music industry would miraculously discover me and offer me a record contract, just as the marketing group at Unisys headquarters in Michigan discovered me in a cubicle on the West Coast. I have heard of this actually happening. You know those stories about an unknown musician quietly playing an original composition at church when a famous producer walks in and discovers this amazing talent? Well, I thought perhaps such a miracle would happen in my life.

The part I didn't know was that the vast majority of these so-called overnight sensations worked for many years to improve their craft and prepare for the moment when performance meets opportunity. These artists also tended to put themselves in places music industry folks scout: showcases, songwriting conferences, singing competitions, and studios. That was exactly what Dave, Cathy, and Debbie had done. Their successes came after many years of diligence and hard work.

I neither prepared for nor sought opportunity. Rather, I buried my talent in the dirt, where it earned not a cent of interest. I frittered away time and squandered the gifts God gave me to use for his purpose.

I decided to put an end to that. I was ready to start living dangerously.

BIRTH PANGS OF SONG, ALBUM, AND MINISTRY

You have searched me, LORD, and you know me.
You know when I sit and when I rise; you perceive my thoughts
from afar. You discern my going out and my lying down;
you are familiar with all my ways. Before a word is on my tongue you,
LORD, know it completely. You hem me in behind and before,
and you lay your hand upon me. Such knowledge is
too wonderful for me, too lofty for me to attain.

PSALM 139:1–6

*J*unko, you need a song on this album that really represents who you are." Cathy took another bite of the cheddar cheese–flavored rice cake, her snack of choice when songwriting.

It was the summer of 1992. We were spread out on Cathy's living room floor in Moreno Valley, California, hard at work on my very first album.

It was my dream-come-true project, and I had spent countless hours gathering songs and rehearsing. We were nearly ready to go into the studio to start recording the album, which Cathy's husband, Dave, would be producing.

But Cathy and Dave felt I needed one last song to make this album complete. As respected veterans of the contemporary Christian music industry, they knew what they were talking about. They've made their living as professional musicians since the early days of the "Jesus movement," and their résumé is quite impressive.

"What do you think about a song with an Oriental feel?" Cathy asked.

What did *I* think? I was just a computer professional/musician wannabe with big dreams and some extra cash, enough to finance a custom album. Everything about the project was new and delightful to me. I felt that I didn't have a worthwhile opinion to offer in response to Cathy's question.

At the same time, something inside me definitely resisted her suggestion. I wondered where that stubborn feeling came from. "I'm not sure, Cathy," I said slowly. "I don't want to get stereotyped."

"Stereotyped? No, Junko, it's not about that. You have a wonderful heritage that makes you unique, and we want to feature that in a song."

"A wonderful heritage"? "Feature that in a song"? As in, draw people's attention to the fact that I'm Japanese? I blanched at the thought.

I had spent my entire American life trying to assimilate into this culture. The last thing I wanted was to make people focus on the fact that I'm different. As though, if I never mentioned in a concert that I'm Asian, no one would ever notice....

After Cathy and I discussed this dilemma at length, it became obvious that, as a Christian artist, I needed to have something to say. I needed to tell my own story. Plenty of Christians can sing— in fact, I once heard someone joke that there are more Christian singers than there are Christians—but God does not call everyone who can sing into the ministry of music. What sets apart those who are called from those who aren't is...their message.

Frankly, at that point I didn't know what my message was.

Aside from the obvious message of the gospel of Jesus Christ, I had only a vague notion of what I wanted to say. I realized I would have credibility only if I spoke from, if not about, my own experience. That meant I couldn't speak on topics such as parenting, overcoming alcohol addiction, prison ministry, or what it's like to be a Christian Super Bowl champion. At that point in my life, I hadn't had firsthand experience with any of those things—and some of them I never will. But those topics, as unfamiliar as they were, felt safer than talking about my real self.

Cathy, however, was convinced that my message ought to have something to do with being Asian American. I preferred to explore my overachieving tendencies and people-pleasing nature. Perhaps we were more in agreement that day than we realized.

At any rate, we needed to find out more about who I was.

On this bridge I walk over the water
Koi fish in the pond...

It was two weeks later that Cathy shared with me the opening lines she had written for my "testimony song." Her husband, Dave, in addition to being a world-class drummer, was also an excellent arranger and producer, and he had come up with a basic track that definitely had an Asian feel to it.

While Dave and Cathy had made some nice progress in two weeks, I had not. *Koi fish? Please! Why don't we add some lotus leaves floating there too?* But I bit my tongue.

"I don't know about the koi pond thing, Cathy."

"Well, how about the next section?" Cathy continued.

A *tiny child running through the rice field*
In the Land of the Rising Sun
A *tiny kite lifting up to heaven*
Touch the face of the Holy One.

Hm. I liked the kite flying and the rice fields. Looked like Cathy really took notes when she asked me about my childhood. "Well," I said, "I like the word picture of the little girl at play. But do you think we could take out the phrase *Land of the Rising Sun?* That's code for Japan, right?"

Cathy sighed. She gently set down her spiral-bound notebook filled with lyric ideas. Then she took a pencil, drew a heart with a lock on the page, and said something I'll never forget.

"Junko, I feel like this is you. It seems like your heart is locked up, and for some reason you won't open it. Why are you doing this? What are you afraid of?"

Honestly, I did not have a good answer. I was digging in my heels whenever Cathy brought up my Japanese heritage, but I didn't exactly know why.

Unless I opened up a little, we were not going anywhere with this song and possibly with the project itself. I was glad when the bag of rice cakes was empty and our songwriting session was over.

As I stood to leave, I promised Cathy that I'd work on this song during my trip to Estes Park, Colorado, where I would be attending a weeklong Christian music seminar.

FOR MANY YEARS ESTES PARK HOSTED A gospel music con-ference with seminars, workshops, concerts, and, of course, singing and vocal competitions. The Estes Park YMCA campgrounds, where we stayed, are located in the heart of the Rocky Mountains, surrounded by some of God's most beautiful handiwork.

But I was so focused on attending all the classes and every concert that I didn't really notice the magnificent backdrop. I might as well have been in New York City! *At least then,* I griped to myself, *I wouldn't have to deal with this high altitude. It's hard to sing my best during the vocal competition.*

Fortunately, David had joined me for this trip. While he golfed during the day, I attended classes on songwriting and stage performance. At the nightly concerts, I got to see live performances by just about every major CCM artist around—Amy Grant, Michael W. Smith, Steven Curtis Chapman, and the list went on.

But what I was really focused on were the competitions. I entered one vocal competition and submitted a song in the songwriting contest.

When I looked around at my fellow competitors, I rather quickly realized they were totally out of my league. This was a particular subculture of performers, mostly singers from the Midwest—and every single one was blond, wore heavy makeup, and sang in a certain style.

Then there were the songwriters. They were definitely a different breed, mostly cerebral types. But I could tell that most of the best writers already knew one another from years of attending conferences together. They also knew how to put together songs that had a "current" sound.

I felt so out of place and so foreign. In fact, I felt acutely self-conscious and very Japanese.

Not surprisingly, I didn't do very well in either competition. I didn't even make it past the first round to the semifinals. Doubts filled my mind: *What is an amateur like me doing trying to record a custom album? I can't sing very well and I can't even write a decent song. Who do I think I am, to believe I'm going to make it?*

I had just poured all my savings into this album project. Was I going to end up with a bunch of silver vanity discs to give away for people to use as coasters?

Frustrated, I decided to go for a run. But running in that thin air and high altitude made me even more irritated, so I asked David to meet me in the car at a restaurant at the bottom of the hill about five miles away. It would be nice to just run downhill, using gravity to my advantage, and then enjoy a dinner out.

I headed out the front gates of the campground, dodging girls squealing with delight about making it past the preliminary round of the competition.

When I first started running, I was simply putting one foot in front of the other, trying not to let negative thoughts drag me down. But after about a mile, the endorphins kicked in.

Soon I ceased feeling sorry for myself and began to think about the song Cathy was helping me write (to be fair, at this point she was the only one writing it). I asked myself why I was so set against focusing on my Japanese self, so reluctant to touch upon that theme in my song—and in my life.

I hadn't thought about my childhood in Japan for years. Then Cathy started asking questions, all in an effort to help me figure out who this artist Junko is and what she's all about.

As I HIT THE TWO-MILE MARK, MY MIND drifted back to the summer when we moved from Osaka to New York. I could almost see my eight-year-old self staring out the window of our red-brick, high-rise apartment in the Bronx, wishing like crazy that I could go back to running around the rice fields again.

Then my best friend in Fujiidera—Yukako—came to mind. In Japan, we played together almost every day after school. She was so nice and so popular, and in second grade she chose *me* as her best friend! When I played with Yukako, we could just be ourselves and have such a good time.

I didn't find a friend like her in New York. Instead, I was surrounded by snobby Tokyo-bred girls. I often yearned for one more chance to fly kites with Yukako in our rice fields. In the chaos of my family's summertime move, I hardly got to say good-bye to her....

In New York, my parents were having a hard enough time adjusting to a new country and concerned about their three daughters. So I kept my disappointments to myself. After all, as we say in Japan, *shikataganai* ("It can't be helped"). You accept life as it comes and move on.

I never shed a tear when we left Japan, because good Japanese girls don't cry. I also didn't cry three years later when we up and moved again, this time to California. I figured friends come and go, so I had to hold them loosely.

My one constant I had—my friend and steady companion—was music. In my heart day and night, my music kept me encouraged. When, for instance, I was unable to speak the language of the people around me. In fact, music had always been my passport to friendship and a ticket to a new environment.

Around the three-mile mark, it came to me that my Japanese-ness was often a source of shame. In the U.S., I was embarrassed and even ashamed not to speak English. Being Japanese was what made me different from everyone else when I desperately wanted to fit in. I hated when people teased me about being Japanese, even when their teasing was in fun.

And here was the clincher: I was sure that if I weren't Japanese, all my problems would go away. But I had imagined for years that music would be my ticket out of this misery. After all, my music set me apart from being just another Japanese girl; I could let that identity prop me up.

But I've learned here at Estes Park that I'm not really a musician after all. I don't stand out as a singer. My songs aren't even good enough to get me past the preliminary round.

The conclusion I drew hit hard: *All this time, I've been chasing a pipe dream.*

That's when the tears started.

I was embarrassed by my tearful reaction. This was my response to losing some dumb music competition? Of course it's disappointing to be told you're not good enough. But I knew very well that there would be many other competitions to enter. I also knew I had lots of room for improvement.

No, my tears were about something else.

I was finally mourning the loss of my childhood. I was grieving those years of carefree ease that I had left behind in Japan. At last I was crying the tears I had never shed when I yearned for life in Osaka, for a childhood season cut short.

I was crying the tears I'd held back when missing Yukako. It was more than twenty years since I'd moved away from Japan, but this was the first time I felt the emotions of the experience. I slowed down to a walk so I wouldn't trip on the blurry road ahead. I couldn't remember the last time I'd cried like this!

When I was a child, my method of coping was to cover it up with my achievements and accomplishments. Having learned to avoid tears at all cost, I tried to be a world-class people pleaser. I let other people's approval numb the pain.

But inside, just beneath the surface, was this constant yearning: *I want to go home!*

When I met the Lord, some of that yearning began to subside. But in another way it increased. I once longed to be back in Osaka, but my year in Japan revealed that my homeland as I remembered it no longer existed.

I didn't really belong in Japan anymore. I didn't belong in America either. I didn't have a place I could truly call home.

Then it dawned on me. As a Christ-follower, I'm yearning for a *new* homeland, for a place I have never even visited. And if playing in the rice fields with Yukako was the most carefree life I will ever experience on earth, how much better will life in my heavenly home be!

There will be no more sorrow; there will be no more tears. *I'm homesick for my future home in heaven*, I realized, and as I started running again, I felt that longing more acutely than I ever had.

As I continued down the hill, flying past the four-mile mark, these words came to me:

I have crossed the bridge over the ocean
  Never said good-bye
To the little girl I left behind
  She had no time to cry
A tiny child lost among the strangers
  In the Land of the Rising Sun
A simple prayer lifting up to heaven
  Touch the heart of the Holy One.

That's it! The reason I couldn't write this song was because I hadn't mourned my lost life in Japan. Just as I never said a proper good-bye to Yukako, I never properly mourned that part of my childhood.

Now, for the first time, I let myself grieve; I allowed the tears to come. In doing so, I found the key that unlocked my heart, and the words began to flow along with the tears.

Then something else magical happened: suddenly I noticed the beauty of my surroundings. I had been in the Colorado Rockies for four days now, and I had not noticed how tall the peaks all around me were, or how green the trees. I hadn't heard the birds singing or seen the sapphire-blue sky.

This place was absolutely gorgeous! Why didn't I noticed its beauty before? How could I have missed it?

I stood for a moment looking at the flowery field beside the road and just savored the beauty of God's creation. *Thank you, Lord. You are so good!*

A rumble of thunder came from somewhere over the distant mountain peaks, signifying an approaching storm. Strangely enough, though, I was unafraid. The sound of thunder no longer held its awful grip of fear on me. Instead, it now served as a tangible reminder of God's magnificence and power.

I continued jogging the last few yards, soaking in the presence of this awesome God, the wonderful Mr. Thunder.

By the time I joined David at the car, in my mind I had finished writing "Land of the Rising Sun," the song that has since become my signature song. David had no idea I had just run the most therapeutic five miles in my life. We had a lot of catching up to do over dinner!

WHEN WE NEXT GOT TOGETHER, CATHY WAS delighted to see how much progress I had made. Here are the full lyrics to the "Land of the Rising Sun":

On this bridge I walk over the water
Searching for some peace
Memories of the life I left behind
I look to the east
A tiny child running through the rice field
In the Land of the Rising Sun
A tiny kite lifting up to heaven
Touch the face of the Holy One
From the Land of the Rising Sun
Into this place I've come
Inside of me there will always be
The Land of the Rising Sun
I have crossed the bridge over the water
Never said good-bye
To the little girl I left behind
She had no time to cry
A tiny child lost among the strangers
Walking under the Risen Son
A simple prayer lifting up to heaven
Touch the heart of the Holy One
(spoken in Japanese, then English)
主イエスキリストよ、いつまでも貴方と友に歩きます。
Lord Jesus
I will walk with You forever
From the Land of the Rising Sun
Into my heart You've come
Inside of me there will always be
The land of the Rising Son
(repeat)*

_____

* *The Land of the Rising Sun*, words and music by Dave & Cathy Spurr and Junko Cheng, copyright 1993 Parbar Music (ASCAP)/Everyday Hero Music (ASCAP), printed with permission, all rights reserved.

At last—and thanks in large part to Cathy and Dave—I finished recording my first album, *No Secrets*, in December 1992. Thus began my journey as a contemporary Christian musician. I leaned upon the contacts I'd developed over the years to book myself at churches, coffee houses, camps, luncheons, and other events throughout Southern California.

At first reluctant to share "Land of the Rising Sun," I would simply mention that it was my testimony song. When the music started, however, something palpable always happened in the room: I could tell that people were deeply touched by the music and the lyrics.

So I worked on a three-minute testimony to introduce the song, and now I sing "Land of the Rising Sun" just about every time I'm in concert. There is something transcendent about this song, and I often hear comments like these from listeners:

I just want you to know that your song about the little girl flying a kite really moved me. I came from another country myself as a young person, and you helped put into words all that I was feeling.

– – –

My wife and I were on the verge of a divorce when we attended your concert and you sang your song "Land of the Rising Sun." For the first time, I pictured my wife as a little girl playing so freely in her home country China. Then I began to be convicted about my putting so much stress and burden on her during this time in our marriage. We confessed to each other that night after we got home and vowed to work on our relationship. I just want you to know that we are now proud parents of two beautiful children, and your song helped us get here.

– – –

I have a neighbor who is from Japan, and when I played your song to her, she started weeping. Now she is going to church with me. Thank you.

– – –

I just moved from Rhode Island, and I want you to know that your song blessed
me. I think I'm going to make it at my new school now.

– – –

And there are more.

Initially, I was surprised that such a personal song could have
such a universal impact, but the feeling of being an outsider is apparently more common than I'd ever imagined.

I have sung "Land of the Rising Sun" in Brazil, Australia,
Canada, Japan, and even Africa. I am continually awed and amazed
by how the Holy Spirit works through this song to bring healing to
people's hearts.

And I was about to be further amazed. You see, I had no idea
how else God would use this song in my life.

10

To Nashville
and Beyond

Many are the plans in a person's heart,
but it is the Lord's purpose that prevails.

PROVERBS 19:21

*T*he contemporary Christian music scene was born of the "Jesus Movement" that swept through Southern California in the late 1960s and into the '70s. As a result, most of the record companies that catered to this new genre were initially based in the Los Angeles area. By the end of the '80s, though, many of those labels had moved to Tennessee. Nashville became the mecca of gospel and contemporary Christian music.

That meant Nashville was home to the Gospel Music Association (GMA). I heard about the association's annual springtime convention for years, but it wasn't until 1993 that I worked up the courage to attend GMA Week. In my opinion, it was a more industry-centric affair than the artist-focused Estes Park seminar.

With my first CD now in hand, I was ready to do business. It was time to scope out the industry landscape for myself.

Thousands of people attended GMA Week in 1993. I walked

around the lobby of the Renaissance Hotel in downtown Nashville feeling, once again, like a total neophyte. Good thing David joined me on this trip too! Otherwise, I wouldn't have known a single soul.

All the industry folks seemed to be friends with one another. They probably worked on the same city block and played church softball together. I sensed a genuine camaraderie—I don't know if it's characteristic of the South or because they were mostly Christians in the Christian music business. It was a nice surprise, and it rendered the universality of the "industry handshake" much more amusing: two people would be happily shaking hands and greeting each other, all the while looking past the other's shoulder to see what more important person might be walking by. Nicer folks genuinely tried to maintain eye contact, but within seconds even they were scanning the room for the next Very Important Person.

The genre of CCM had been increasing its piece of the music industry pie and by 1993 had surpassed jazz, New Age, and classical. I saw big-name Christian artists sauntering around with their handlers, usually heading into temporary radio booths to do interviews.

Giveaways were everywhere—pens, mugs, caps, T-shirts, books, CDs, and magazines. I had to pace myself if I wanted to close my suitcase at the end of the week.

This Gospel Music Week conference did have a track for no-name—oops, I mean *unsigned*—artists like me, and the organizers treated us very kindly. There were luncheons, meet-and-greets, training sessions, and outings to places like record companies and bookstores so we could learn more about the now multimillion-dollar Christian music industry.

I enjoyed meeting other independent artists from around the country, but we were definitely on the outside looking in. It shouldn't have surprised me that this conjured up memories of my first day as a freshman at Foothill High School. I had vivid flashbacks of walking around campus, seeing the popular football players hanging around the beautiful cheerleaders.

I felt completely invisible.

When I made the leap from office cubicle to full-time music career, I learned that there were two basic approaches: the independent ("indie") way or the industry way. Not having experience with or knowledge of either, I decided to test the waters in both ponds.

I called churches, booked myself to sing locally, and worked to gain grassroots support as an indie. I kept pretty busy this way.

But I also wanted to explore the possibility of having the industry behind me. Very few people get signed to a label, but those who do have an immediate advantage over indies: big record companies with large budgets. This provides a means for recording, marketing, and sending on the road to open for bigger artists.

My chances of getting signed by a label were slim, I knew that. But *someone* always wins the lottery; why couldn't it be me?

IN THE MONTHS LEADING UP TO GMA Week, I sent copies of my CD to various record companies. When I heard that one of the optional outings for us was a tour of one of those record companies, I signed up.

While David explored a scenic golf course in the Nashville area, I hopped aboard the air-conditioned coach with a group of other newbies.

We enjoyed a scenic drive through downtown Nashville and into the suburbs before pulling up to an ornate building in Brentwood.

Our footsteps reverberated into the marble lobby. So many top names in the Christian music industry entered this building every day! Framed gold and platinum records by current artists hung on the walls, commemorating number one hit singles through the years. I had grown up on those songs; I was awestruck.

The tour guide led us to the artist and repertoire (A&R) division. This is the heart and soul of a record company. A&R are the ones who discover and sign artists. They also develop the talent and help with the entire recording process.

As I passed the cubicle of the assistant to the top A&R guy, I spotted something familiar: my CD! The one I had sent to this record company was sitting on his desk.

In excitement, I ran over to see if they had actually opened it. *Did they listen to it? Did they like it?* As I got closer, I saw a handwritten note scrawled on a Post-It. I couldn't believe what it said: "Nothing special."

My CD. *Nothing special?*

Thousands of my hard-earned dollars had gone into this project. Cathy and Dave put countless hours and immeasurable love and care into choosing songs, arranging music, hiring musicians, and producing that album. I had shed tears over "Land of the Rising Sun." Singing those songs had been a life-changing experience. Everyone who heard my album loved it—or so they told me. *This is very special!*

I was crushed. I felt like a mom who's just been told her kid is ugly. I wanted to grab that CD and hide it in my bag—or at least peel off the sticky note and replace it with one that said, "Very special! *Must* listen!"

But instinct took over. I ran away from that desk as if I had seen a dead rat. My new friends asked me what was wrong. I tried to say calmly, "Oh, nothing."

Yeah, nothing. Nothing special.

$\mathcal{C}$HE BUS RIDE BACK TO THE CONVENTION center was ago-
nizing, but I needed to stay positive. It was almost time for the vocal
competition.

Before arriving at GMA, I thought I'd had it with competitions.
But when they asked for sign-ups during the luncheon on the first
day, I couldn't resist. This contest had a twist: we would be indi-
vidually videotaped performing our song and then evaluated by an
industry professional.

This competition definitely had its positives. I liked the idea of
the videotape and professional critique of my performance.

I decided to go for uniqueness. Certain that no one else in
Nashville would sing about flying a kite on the rice fields in Japan,
I walked into the appointed room later that afternoon carrying my
background tracks for "Land of the Rising Sun." To my great relief, I
saw that my professional evaluator was Tom Jackson.

Tom is a stage performance coach—a rarity in the Christian
music industry. I remembered him from a workshop I attended at
Estes Park the previous summer. He was smart, insightful, and very
tactful when critiquing a performer.

So why a performance coach? Because a lot of Christian singers sound great but look no better than a flagpole onstage. No one
has the nerve to tell them the truth; all they hear at church is how
wonderful they sound or how much they blessed the congregation.

Artists (yes, myself included) often have no real clue what cues
we send with our body language. Tom has the rare ability to bring
out the best in each performer by speaking truth in love—with a
good dose of humor. (Only a few years into this career at that time,
Tom has since proven to the Christian music world and the music
industry at large that his method works. Some of his more successful
clients include Taylor Swift, Casting Crowns, and Jars of Clay.)

Before we began, Tom positioned me in front of a simple back-drop. Then he cued the videographer as my song started. When I finished, he was silent for a moment.

Darn it, I thought. *I chose the wrong song!*

Then Tom started talking. He loved it! He asked me about my life and how the song came to be. Then he encouraged me to take my performance a step further: "Why don't you sing it as if you are a Japanese dancer wearing a kimono, and pretending that you have one of those silk fans in your hands?"

Wow, we are going for the jugular! By this point in my life, though, I was past any sense of shame about being Japanese. I felt ready to embrace it.

Tom gave me a few other pointers, such as raising my arm slowly to indicate the rising of the sun, moving my gaze across the room as if from the east to the west, and pretending to fly a kite.

I would never have thought of these things. Under Tom's guid-ance, I practiced a few times until I felt comfortable. Then we did another video take. Afterward, when Tom scored my performance, he insisted on giving me an extremely high score to ensure me a spot in the top ten.

My twenty minutes were over all too quickly. I walked out with a grateful heart and a lot more confidence than I'd had just a few hours earlier.

AT THE END OF THE NEXT DAY, the list of the top ten finalists was posted—and my name was on it! The organizers called a quick meeting to instruct us about the live performances the next evening and to read the names of the industry professionals who would be on the judging panel. I couldn't believe I would actually be performing in front of these well-known movers and shakers in the CCM world.

My mind raced. *This is it! I'll get a record deal, go on tour, and finally recoup all the money I invested in this CD project.*

Later that day I went for a run along Church Street to the Vanderbilt University campus. As I ran, I thought about how quickly things had changed since that morning. But I felt ready for whatever adventure God had in store.

The next evening, everyone gathered in the historic Ryman Auditorium and listened to the emcee introduce the dignitaries and judges. As each contestant sang, I was struck by how unique every vocal performance was. *If God has been working on all of these artists just as he has me, then he has been really busy!* I was blessed by each performance.

Then it was my turn. I took my place onstage and the music began. As usual, I sensed that people were sincerely moved by the song. I myself was almost overwhelmed by emotion as I did my best at imitating a Japanese dancer, as Tom had suggested.

When I sang the last note and the music ended, a moment passed. Then the auditorium erupted in applause.

During a short intermission, the judges tallied our scores. Then they announced the names of the third- and second-place winners. I hadn't heard my name yet; I had either not impressed the judges or won the competition.

Based on the way the crowd was looking at me and smiling, I had a strange feeling that I might just have eked out the win. At that moment, it hardly mattered. I got to perform before key industry people; the heads of four or five major Christian record companies were among the judges.

Then the announcer called the name of the winner of the Video Critique Competition for GMA 1993.

It was me.

As I hugged my husband and bounded up the steps to accept the award, the crowd gave me a standing ovation. I could see Tom Jackson's face in the crowd—he was beaming at me. It was a glorious moment.

I felt so validated and so…vindicated. *"Nothing special"? I am something special!*

YOU MIGHT THINK THAT AFTER THIS HONOR, I got a record deal, went on tour, and had a couple number one hits. You might think—as the culture and media often imply—that dreams really do come true. That you can be all you want to be if you work hard enough or only believe.

Well, things don't always turn out the way we expect or even hope. With the benefit of hindsight, I realize that what has happened since that day—and more important, what has *not* happened—was the best path for me.

Oh, I definitely experienced major highs and lows during that one week in Nashville during the spring of 1993. That was only the first of many such ups and downs as I pursued my musical career.

After winning the GMA vocal competition, I was offered a record deal on the spot. However, it was with a small record company in the niche market of Southern gospel. As much as I appreciated their belief in me and the kind offer, I declined. I just didn't feel I was a good fit. I was also holding out for an offer from one of the top three or four major labels.

One such record company did show interest, and I even met and spent a day with the A&R person there. John Mays is a brilliant man with a knack for discovering unknown artists who go on to become major CCM artists: Point of Grace, Cindy Morgan, and Nichole Nordeman. John saw potential in me, but after our day together he decided not to pursue me further.

"Junko," he said, "you have a unique quality about you that is very intriguing. You have a way of creating fans all around you. You have a good voice—a great voice, actually. But it just doesn't have the excellence to make it on the radio."

He paused. "Now, I've been wrong before. I passed on a few other artists"—here he mentioned the names of two or three artists who eventually became top acts on other labels, and I saw a shadow of regret on his face—"so I might be sorry for letting you go. But know this. Philippians 1:6 says, 'He who began a good work in you will carry it on to completion until the day of Christ Jesus.' If God has truly called you into this ministry, he will use you. It might not be in the industry I work in, but you will carry on. In fact, you really don't need us at all! Now, get out there and go kick up some dust."

I was disappointed to get so close yet still be rejected. However, John's words proved a source of great encouragement. I appreciated his straightforwardness and honesty. He affirmed my conviction that God called me to this ministry and that, whether I got a record deal or not, God would use me.

I truly appreciated that John took time to talk with me. Today he and I are still friends; we stay in touch, and he remains one of my biggest cheerleaders.

Another artist-manager—a Brit named Dave with a pretty wife from Hawaii—also took an interest in me at the competition. For a while, he pursued me. Dave had somehow ended up in Nashville, and at the time we met, he was managing a couple of pretty famous artists. I considered having him manage my career, but he insisted that I move to Nashville. "Junko, if you really want to make it in the

CCM world, you have to live where everything happens. California is too far away, and once you're out of sight, you will be out of mind. You have to be seen."

Moving to Nashville was out of the question for David and me. Our Southern California roots ran deep, and David was just starting his medical practice. This would have been a terrible time to uproot.

We briefly considered my getting an apartment in Nashville and living there part-time while commuting back and forth. But the idea of living apart did not appeal to us. Eventually we decided against a move to Nashville, after which time Dave lost interest and the phone stopped ringing.

Today, David and I look back on that decision with no regret. Actually, with great relief! Too many couples we know are no longer married because they chose physical distance. Out of sight, out of mind—indeed!

The more I learned about the reality of the CCM music industry, the more unappealing it became to me. If I *had* gotten a great record deal, touring would have kept David and me apart for months.

At that time I had no idea the extent to which artists sacrifice to go on tour. Getting signed is just the beginning; there's still a long way to go before a record hits the charts—and at what personal cost to the artist?

Furthermore, the thought of living out of a suitcase and sleeping on a tour bus did not sound glamorous to me. I'm a bit of a homebody, and as you already know, I like my routine. My guess is that many touring artists prefer normal life too, but either they are truly called to minister in this way or they get caught up in the machine.

Certainly, many contemporary Christian artists somehow survive this lifestyle with their sanity and their marriages intact; but I know too many former artists who didn't. I might easily have wound up in that camp.

I also realized I had a few things working against me. First, I was probably too old to be signed as a freshman artist. I was over thirty, and I needed to be about ten years younger for anyone to consider signing me, a newbie. And that is just one of the advantages to being young in this business.

Another advantage of youth is being better equipped to keeping up a pace that is taxing physically and mentally—touring and singing night after night.

Younger people are also more malleable, so music industry handlers can groom them. I was too set in my ways—and I had much stronger opinions about things than they wanted to deal with!

And because young people are often single and without kids, they have the freedom to pour their time and energy into music. Once an artist becomes established, it is easier to make family life a higher priority. But until then, it is difficult to give anything less than 100 percent to the demands of the music and the road trips.

The marketing machinery at every label invests thousands of dollars in a new artist, and that artist wants to see the label's gamble pay off. If it doesn't, artists know it's out the door they go. I've known more than a few singers who feel chewed up and spit out by the whole CCM machine.

As real and significant as these negatives were, I might have overcome them. But I knew from my experience at Estes Park that I was only so-so vocally. Yes, I'm a good singer, perhaps even very good within my own circle. But to make it at the national level, I had to be better. Much, much better.

I have since done more vocal training and strengthened my

voice, but there are limits to what I can do with my God-given talent. And I just can't do enough.

That said, even weak vocals can be overcome if an artists demonstrates great songwriting ability. But I was still a budding songwriter. I didn't have a catalog of original songs to impress industry folks with.

Evidently, most of Nashville agreed that "Land of the Rising Sun" was brilliant. They just wanted more of it. And all I had were run-of-the-mill CCM songs that could have been sung by any other Christian female artist on the circuit.

Ironically, this is exactly what I wanted back when I started choosing songs with Dave and Cathy: to sing "vanilla" tunes that wouldn't give away my ethnicity. Now that plan was backfiring!

I've since developed my songwriting skills, too. Sometimes I wonder if my songs would have been good enough if I'd had them back in Nashville.

WHEN THE MUSIC TRENDS BEGAN TO SHIFT. In 1994, the year after I won the GMA Video Critique Competition, grunge became the hot sound in the Christian music scene. That meant every person working in the CCM industry was now on the lookout for the hottest bands with guitar-wielding guys playing Nirvana-esque music. And that meant I sang not only the wrong genre, but was the wrong gender.

I did attend GMA again the next year, and once again there was a new artist competition. Unlike the previous year, though, the name of the competition was a whole lot catchier: Spotlight '94. When I tell people that I won the competition in 1993, I say that I won Spotlight '93 even though that title technically didn't exist.

Everyone's forgotten about the Video Critique Competition, but no one forgets Spotlight '94 because of the following success story:

At the orientation meeting for the Spotlight '94 competition, the organizers introduced me to the eager contestants as the previous year's winner. The guys in a band sitting near me turned around to introduce themselves. They were from a college in North Carolina, excited to be at GMA for the first time, and thrilled to meet me. They even asked me for my autograph. When I asked what their band's name was, they told me Jars of Clay.

You can probably guess the rest of the story. Jars of Clay won the Spotlight '94 competition that year, were immediately signed, and hit the road soon after. Since each was young and single, they could pack their bags without hesitation. Those young men were at the right place at the right time, and their sound was all the rage.

When I saw them again at GMA in 1995, they were just releasing their first album with a smallish record label. When they spotted me in the lobby, they came up and excitedly showed me their new PR kit. They were still just as sweet as ever, and I couldn't help but root for them. I wished them well as they left to do a showcase at an industry luncheon.

Nobody imagined that "Flood," their first single, would not only become a breakout hit in Christian music but catch on like wildfire in the mainstream music industry as well. Their video was an MTV mainstay for months, and Jars of Clay became a household name.

Tom Jackson has obviously done a great job working on their stage presence. But most of all, I am happy that they stayed grounded despite all of their success. A few years ago, they found my website and wrote a nice note in my guestbook: "Hey, Junko! Just wanted to see what's up. Good to see you're still out there. Love, the Jars guys."

TO THIS DAY, I OCCASIONALLY THINK about the what-ifs:

What if I had embarked on my music career when I was younger?

What if David and I had moved to Nashville?

What if I had come to terms with my Japanese ethnicity earlier and written more songs embracing that identity?

What if I could sing better?

What if I had continued to pursue other record deals instead of giving up after my conversation with John?

What if I had accepted the first offer from the smaller label?

Fortunately, these questions don't keep me up at night. I have learned over the years just how true Philippians 1:6 is. God who began a good work in me has indeed been carrying on that work in and through me.

I have sung at thousands of churches all around the globe. I have shared my testimony with many people. In 1993, I never guessed how many places I would one day visit. I've performed all over the US, in Japan, Australia, Brazil, Canada, and other countries.

In Hawaii, I had a surprise hit on KAIM radio that went to number two; I even heard myself on the radio a few times while traveling in Honolulu! Let me tell you, that's a thrill like no other. I wanted to roll down my car window and scream at all the drivers around me to turn on the radio because THAT'S ME!

Who would have known I would become one of Hawaii's top "local artists" and be invited to open for Michael W. Smith and Avalon when they came through the Islands on their concert tours?

After David and I became parents, I continued to see God's faithful and ongoing work in and through me. I was able to adjust my schedule to spend less time on the road and more at home.

Then, several years ago, I switched my focus to children's music. I now enjoy performing for kids and their parents. I've also added worship leading to my repertoire, and I often lead worship at churches, retreats, and Bible studies.

These kinds of career decisions don't require consulting my label, agent, manager, and promoter. I don't have handlers fussing all around me. I simply consult God, David, and myself!

I still perform—often within driving distance of home while the kids are at school, or on a weekend fly-date. I still write songs and record, and most people make no distinction between signed and unsigned artists.

Bottom line, people get to listen to music that ministers to them, and all of that comes from God.

I have a family that I love and enjoy very much. I had no idea back in 1993 that God already had a custom-tailored plan for my music—and, in fact, my life. We serve a God who is gracious, wise, and so very good.

THE MUSIC INDUSTRY IS DEFINITELY an inexact science. There are countless hits and misses for everyone involved. If I think I have made more than my share of questionable decisions about the CCM music industry, I'm somewhat comforted to know that even knowledgeable veterans like John Mays occasionally miss…

He passed on Jars of Clay.

11

My Brazil Adventure

When you pass through the waters,
I will be with you;
and when you pass through the rivers,
they will not sweep over you.
When you walk through the fire,
you will not be burned;
the flames will not set you ablaze.
For I am the LORD, your God,
the Holy One of Israel, your Savior.

ISAIAH 43:1–2

My music has enabled me to travel to many cities across the U.S. and abroad. I feel fortunate to have already been to more places than most people go in their entire lifetime!

So why, then, was I nervous about a three-week concert tour through Brazil in July of 1995? It wasn't because of safety concerns. I would be traveling with a group from Japanese Evangelical Missionary Society (JEMS), a missions organization that has been sending short- and long-term workers overseas for years.

Most missions trips to Brazil are to teach English, work at camps with kids, and help run vacation Bible school. Deciding to do something fun and different, John Katagi, the director of South American Missions for JEMS, invited me to perform concerts in several cities throughout Brazil. John and his staff arranged for me to stay with host families in the various Brazilian cities where I would be performing concerts; they even lined up a young woman named Patricia to be my translator and companion for the trip. I knew I would be safe and well taken care of.

Was the language barrier the biggest hurdle? No. I was only partially concerned about my inability to speak Portuguese. We would have a few weekend training sessions prior to the trip, and John was going to offer intensive language classes.

Of course, I knew I wouldn't be able to speak this foreign language after just a few lessons. And it didn't help that I kept mixing Portuguese up with what little Spanish I'd heard around California and the little French I remembered from high school. Mostly I concentrated on learning the essentials—"Hi," "Thank you," and "Where is the bathroom?"

Besides, John had shared the somewhat surprising fact that my Japanese would come in handy in Brazil, of all places! Back in the mid-1800s, Japanese farmers began leaving famine-plagued Japan for the more fertile soil of Brazil, resulting in large settlements of Japanese (also known as *Nikkei*) throughout the country. The Nikkeis continued coming to Brazil in waves every few decades, and many of those who immigrated in the mid-1900s still spoke Japanese better than Portuguese. I would be singing primarily at Nikkei churches in Brazil, so, since I had Japanese covered and Patricia spoke Portuguese, communication would not be much of an issue.

Here's the main reason for my hesitation: I had to raise financial support!

This was a concert tour like no other. When I traveled, I usually paid my own way or had the inviting church or organization cover my travel expenses. And in this case, I wouldn't have minded paying for the trip myself. But even factoring in the group discount on airfare and home stays instead of hotel stays, my travel expenses would total $3655. David and I simply could not afford to pay the full amount by ourselves.

Everything in me resisted asking my friends and family to send me on a summertime adventure. How humbling, if not totally humiliating!

David and I were able to contribute substantially to the cost; then I began the arduous task of composing a support letter. You know, the kind we so often receive from teens or college students going on a short-term mission, or from long-time missionary friends who devote their lives to spreading the gospel in remote regions.

Now the roles were reversed. It's very hard to ask for support, I realized. And soon I found myself completely stuck. *How do I write this letter?*

Fortunately, my friend and mentor Sherry Harrah helped clarify some things for me. A support letter, she explained, actually gives people the opportunity to travel with me, in a sense. Most people have too many daily commitments to be able to drop everything and go on a mission trip, even if they want to. I was fortunate to have the time, energy, and now a prospective group of supporters to make this trip possible. Furthermore, Sherry said, a support letter would prevent my being a "lone ranger" missionary. Instead, I would have people personally invested in my trip through prayer and financial contributions.

I so appreciated Sherry's wisdom. After that, I was able to write a letter with more of a "join my team" tone than an "I need your money" feel. To my delight, people immediately responded. Letters poured in to the JEMS office. Some supporters sent a note saying that although they couldn't support me monetarily, they would pray for me. Others sent generous checks. I treasured every reply, no matter the amount. I felt so blessed and loved. To think that I had almost denied myself—and my supporters—this wonderful opportunity!

One other important thing Sherry and her husband, Walt, taught me is the importance of daily Bible reading and quiet time. I understood the need for regular Bible study and weekly sermons. I just didn't realize how much a daily devotional could affect my Christian growth. I now believe that, in the long term, those quiet times contribute more to a growing knowledge of God than almost anything else—even more than hearing a great sermon, attending a weekend spiritual retreat, or praying with a friend or spouse.

Yet a quiet time alone sounds so...unglamorous. Walt and Sherry, however, were instrumental in helping me recognize the invaluable lessons God teaches as we apply Scripture to daily life.

I used to think I needed a pastor or a theologian to translate God's Word for me. In fact, all I need is the Holy Spirit—and he is with me already! The Harrahs recommended a daily Bible reading plan that would take us through the entire Bible in two years, and I faithfully kept to the reading schedule in the days leading up to the trip and throughout my travels.

I was amazed to see God reveal something new daily. It nearly always applied directly to what I was going through, as if he were walking beside me.

*C*HERE WAS ONE OTHER REASON FOR MY reluctance to go on the Brazil trip: I was waiting to hear back from several Japanese record companies that had shown interest in distributing my second album.

I hadn't sought out an opportunity in Japan. But while singing at a Japanese church in LA, I met a man named Jun Tanaka whose brother worked in the entertainment industry in Tokyo. Jun insisted on having his brother shop my CD to Japanese record distributors.

Surprisingly, many of Jun's contacts in Japan remembered me from NHK television. Soon, several major record companies expressed interest and a bidding war began. Jun was calling me weekly with updates, and at one point I traveled to Japan and met with some Sony executives. I began to wonder whether work in Japan was God's next step for me.

Nashville rejected me; this is a nice consolation prize, I thought. Perhaps God was giving me an opportunity to reach a wider audience in Japan, where less than 1 percent of the population is Christian.

Jun had begun drawing up contracts for me to look over and making plans for me to travel more often to Japan. Now, I expected a phone call any day with an offer from one of his top three companies.

Around that same time, I got a call from the executive editor of *Today's Christian Woman*, a premier Christian magazine that has since been absorbed by its parent magazine, *Christianity Today*. At that point, *Today's Christian Woman* had a bimonthly readership of over 750,000 people. The editor had received an enthusiastic recommendation about me after I performed at Willow Creek Community Church in Illinois. She wanted to interview me.

Wow, three-quarters of a million people will be reading about me? That's huge!

Ramona Cramer Tucker flew all the way out to California to

spend two days interviewing me. Another crew flew out some time later for a photo shoot at my home. I couldn't believe a "nobody" like me was getting this kind of treatment. When I told a few people in Nashville, they couldn't believe it either.

Because of this magazine's reach, record companies lobbied to get their artists interviewed. But *TCW* published only six issues a year, a fact that limited the likelihood of landing such an interview. My music industry friends wanted to know how I did it. I could only reply, "I didn't! God did." It was an opportunity truly orchestrated by him.

During our interview, I told Ramona that within weeks I was leaving for Brazil on concert tour and that any day now I expected an offer from one of three major record companies in Tokyo.

It surprised me that Ramona was more interested in character-izing me as an independent artist working in the music industry because it was God's call on my life. In fact, she almost preferred that I didn't have a record company propping me up, and she told me so.

I wasn't sure how to take that at the time. Later, I would see clearly that this woman had great discernment.

ON THE DAY OF MY DEPARTURE FOR Brazil, while I was doing some last-minute packing, the phone rang. It was Jun Tanaka.

He broke the news to me: all three labels decided independently of one another to walk away. At the same time. He couldn't believe it.

Jun mentioned something about my CD being "religious in nature." We had spoken earlier and thought we cleared that hurdle. Since I was singing in English, listeners wouldn't really understand what I was singing about; the lyrical content didn't matter. The Japanese executives all liked the sound of my voice and the excellent musical arrangements of my producer. Or so I had been told.

And now this.

Lord, why did you tease me like this? I didn't really care if I got a record deal in Japan. This happened just as I was finally letting go of my Nashville dreams. I didn't ask for it. It feels like you got my hopes up for no good reason. What was that all about?

I was trying to process this news when my parents showed up to drive me to the airport instead of David, who couldn't get off work that day. It was time to go.

I stuffed my luggage into the trunk of their car and crawled into the backseat, feeling dejected yet again. My parents were as surprised and disappointed as I to hear the bad news. They had been so certain of a record deal that they had told their friends and relatives in Japan about it.

They tried to find several possible explanations for this unexpected turn of events during our hour-long ride to LAX, but mostly they tried to steer the conversation toward more cheerful topics while I stared out the window.

My dad dropped off my mom and me at the curb so that she could help me check in while he parked the car. While at the ticket counter, I suddenly remembered that I had been asked to prepare some Japanese folk songs to sing to the aging Nikkeis, so they could enjoy some music in their native language. I asked my mom if she would write down the lyrics to some of my favorites that she sang to me as a child in Osaka. Every Japanese knows these songs by heart, and I certainly didn't want to mess up the words!

We pulled out the only piece of paper we could find—the back of the itinerary printout—and she quickly began scribbling the lyrics, all the while mumbling and complaining about being in a rush and not being given enough notice to do this.

I hurried through security and waved good-bye to my parents. After settling down in my seat on the plane, I pulled out the crumpled piece of paper with my mom's Japanese handwriting, rushed yet still beautiful. In between the lines, I swear I could read these invisible words: "We're so proud of you. Don't get discouraged. Darn those record companies."

I held in my hand a tangible evidence of unconditional love and support of a mom who has always been my biggest fan...even if she didn't always appreciate fully what it means for me to be a Christian musician in ministry ("So, does that make you a priest now?"). If she could have sent me off to Brazil with a bowl of rice and some hot miso soup, I'm certain that she would have.

I was ready for my adventure in Brazil!

WHEN WE LANDED IN SAN PAULO, John Katagi greeted the JEMS team members at baggage claim. It had been a long flight through three time zones from LA.

Since most of my international travels take me to either Japan or an English-speaking country like Canada and Australia, I'm not often in a country where I don't understand anything being spoken around me. Good thing John was fluent! He helped us find our host families' homes that first night in Brazil.

As soon as I met Patricia, my translator and "personal assistant" (I liked the sound of that!), I knew I was in good hands. Just twenty-one years old, Patricia seemed mature beyond her age. She spoke excellent English, despite never having been to the U.S. In fact, she had never set foot outside Brazil. Patricia is a Spirit-filled woman, very thoughtful, quite sensitive, and not overly talkative. She also truly has a servant's heart.

The next day we were off to our first stop: Curitiba, a beautiful city in the south of Brazil. I sang at a few venues in the city. Brazilians are very musical, and they love concerts. We were treated like rock stars.

Each of my concerts—in every city we visited—was filled with people who not only stood and clapped enthusiastically to every song, but syncopated their clapping. The Brazilians are generous people, and relationships are much more important to them than material things. I received gifts of all kinds from many in my audience, but they also spent a lot of time trying out their English on me and treating me like an old friend.

And it was a good thing that I was able to sing the old Japanese folk songs, thanks to my mother, because the Nikkei seniors loved them. Their eyes always filled with tears as I sang these traditional songs a capella, transporting them back to their homeland and to a time when their lives were simpler.

Everywhere I went the people were welcoming and friendly; in every city I was blessed by their hospitality. When my hosts in Curitiba asked me what I wanted to do during my downtime, I told them that I'd like to go for a run around the lake at the gorgeous park on the other end of town. As beautiful and relatively safe as Curitiba may be, my hosts didn't think it was a good idea for me to run through the park by myself. So they set me up with a "bodyguard," an athletic young man who would keep me company on my run.

I've already told you that I'm not that great of a runner, but my bodyguard was even less so. By the end of my run, he was exhausted. The next day, I asked my host to take me back to the park for another run, and this time I was met by a team of young people from their church. Word had gotten out that I was a serious runner and they had arranged for a relay team to accompany me! I could barely keep up with the fresh set of legs coming at me every half mile or so. This time, *I* was exhausted.

More than anything, though, I was overwhelmed by the thoughtfulness displayed by everyone I encountered. On we went from Curitiba…on to Campo Grande, Londrina, Belem—a different city every few days.

At every new town, the pastor of the hosting church or our host family would take us out to a Churrascaria (pronounced *shu-has-ka-ria'*), a Brazilian steakhouse. Passadores (meat waiters) show up tableside with knives and a skewer, on which are speared various kinds of meat—beef, pork, filet mignon, lamb, chicken, duck, ham, sausage, fish, or any other local cut of meat. A Churrascaria has delicious food, and it's a festive place for Brazilian celebrations. But the food is very heavy. After our third welcome dinner, it finally caught up with us.

Evidently, Patricia and I were not the only JEMS workers to be treated to Churrascaria restaurants multiple times during our trip. Our running joke became this new definition of the Brazilian steak houses: *Churrascaria* (which rhymes with that typical stomach ailment experienced by travelers) came to mean the thing that happens to your tummy when you have had too much churrascos!

OUR FLIGHTS BETWEEN CITIES WENT SMOOTHLY, and I was having a great time in every city we visited. But a couple of things were heavy on my heart. This was especially true at night, when I should have been sleeping.

I was sad about the Japanese distribution deals that fell through. Negative thoughts haunted me. *See, you* are *a nobody. You are only good enough for the amateur circuit. You can't cut it in the real music industry.* In the still of night, I would toss and turn, trying to pray those thoughts away. They robbed me of self-confidence as well as rest.

The funny thing was that I awoke each morning with a renewed perspective. During the day, negative thoughts didn't even enter my mind. I'd have a wonderful concert and then experience an emotional high, knowing God had used me to minister to yet another group of Brazilians. Then I would return to my room at nighttime and fall asleep, only to be awakened by negative thoughts in the middle of the night.

These extreme up-and-down cycles puzzled me. I remembered that during our JEMS orientation, John Katagi told us that Brazil is a very spiritual place and we shouldn't be surprised if we experienced some strange things. He reminded us that God is also very much at work in the U.S., but we are so blinded by materialism that we don't pay attention to the spiritual warfare all around us. Because of the lack of material trappings in Brazil, one senses the presence of the Spirit a lot more readily. I wondered if this was what John meant.

My sadness over the distribution deal wasn't the only thing weighing heavily on my mind. I was also concerned about a potentially huge glitch in our itinerary. After the concert, I had only a small window of time to catch my flight if I were to get back to Sao Paulo in time to catch my international flight back home.

The main reason it was important is because I was on a very tight travel schedule. You see, once I got home, David and I were flying out almost immediately for a business trip. If I didn't catch my international flight, I would have to wait two more days for the next one, and David and I would miss our travel window altogether.

Unfortunately, my final weekend in Brazil was also a holiday weekend in that country. Every seat on that once-a-day flight from the small town of Belem to Sao Paulo was booked—and then some! In fact, more than sixty people were on the waiting list; I was number twenty-six. This, despite the fact that Liliane, the JEMS administrative assistant to South American missions, had gotten to work on my itinerary as soon as I was cleared by the board to go on this trip.

True to my nature, I got pretty worked up about this situation as the date of my last Brazil concert approached. *David will never want me to travel again if I mess this up!* I thought. He had been so patient in the three weeks I toured Brazil, so supportive of this trip.

So at every church we visited, I asked people to pray about this situation—and they did. Whenever we were at an airport, we stopped by customer service to check on the status of our flight to Sao Paolo. Each time we were told that there was absolutely no change, and that nothing could be done.

Then, two weeks into my trip, a few seats suddenly opened up and Patricia moved up to confirmed status on the flight. I moved up, too...to number twenty-three.

I wasn't afraid to take another flight and travel unaccompanied by Patricia, but there was no other flight except for the one the next day. It would be a day too late. As the days went by, I grew more desperate. My prayers changed from politely asking for God's intervention to screaming for help. It was hard enough to be away from David for three whole weeks. I missed him too badly to go even one extra day longer!

Patricia and I even started thinking about ways to fix the situation ourselves. First, I suggested bribing the airlines officials. I figured that most of the country was run on bribes, anyway. We had heard of Brazilian government officials bribing fellow workers in order to get their way, drivers handing a couple of bills to the police to avoid a traffic ticket (and the police expecting this), and of course customers "tipping" the host at the popular restaurant for the best seat in the house. So why couldn't I slip the airlines worker a few bucks under the ticket counter so he would move my name up the list?

But then that same day I read these words from the Old Testament:

Do not pervert justice or show partiality. Do not accept a bribe, for a bribe blinds the eyes of the wise and twists the words of the righteous. (Deuteronomy 16:19)

Yikes! Okay, so God's clearly telling me that I shouldn't bribe my way onto that flight.

That's when I came up with my second idea: What if Patricia and I switched passports so I could get her seat and she could get mine on that other flight? Both of us are Japanese (she is a fourth-generation Japanese Brazilian), and most people think we all look alike, right?

It might have worked…except that Patricia is about three inches shorter than I am and has a much rounder face. We didn't look alike at all, even if we did have the same hair color. We stood in front of the mirror, shook our heads in unison, and reluctantly handed our passports back to each other.

OUR LAST FULL DAY IN BELEM ARRIVED. I would perform my final concert that night; I was still number twenty-three on the flight waiting list. The possibility of my flying home as scheduled was not looking very likely.

I was frustrated. So many things in my life—my travels, record company deals, my music, and now my flight home—were not working out the way I had planned.

Little did I know the miracle that awaited me.

12

God Is in Control

No king is saved by the size of his army;
no warrior escapes by his great strength.
A horse is a vain hope for deliverance;
despite all its great strength it cannot save.
But the eyes of the Lord are on those who fear him,
on those whose hope is in his unfailing love,
to deliver them from death
and keep them alive in famine.

God richly blessed that final concert in Brazil. Patricia's translation of my testimony was seamless. The crowd was on fire. We all had a great time together.

After the concert ended, I was milling about the product table as usual, talking with people and signing autographs. A lot of people asked about my travel plans, so I told many of them about my flight dilemma.

Then a man came up who spoke pretty good English. I still recall that short conversation as if it happened yesterday. He told me that he had worked for a few years in New York City and recently returned to Belem, his hometown. Then he said, "You know, sometimes God keeps you waiting because he has something better planned for you."

At that moment, it was as if the entire room went silent. All I could hear was that man saying those words. I almost dropped the pen I was holding.

Does he know I've been trying like crazy to get a seat on that plane?

Does he know I was turned down by multiple record companies?

Does he know I've been waiting and waiting for God to do something with my music while I fight to keep seeds of doubt and self-pity from taking root in my heart?

The man took the autographed CD from my hand, thanked me, and disappeared into the crowd. I didn't even get his name. I only vaguely recall what he looked like—Caucasian, dark hair, medium height and build, and possibly wings on his back.

OUR HOSTS UNDERSTOOD MY DILEMMA about the flight. They had called the airlines multiple times, explaining that I had an international flight to catch. All to no avail.

After the concert, our hosts treated us to a final dinner out. (Thankfully, at a non-charrascaria restaurant!) Sometime in the middle of dinner, while the server was refilling our water glasses, the thought came to me: *Do I really think I know better than God his will for my life?*

Suddenly, I realized I had been trying to manipulate something I had no control over. *Maybe God doesn't want me to go on that flight for some reason. Maybe it's going to crash! Maybe he's trying to protect me from something terrible.*

I had been trying to force my way onto the flight. Not only

that, but I had almost resorted to bribing and cheating! *How dare I think that I know better than God what his will for my life ought to be? How stupid to think I could do any good by taking matters into my own hands.*

Initially struck by shame, then overwhelmed by God's goodness in caring for and protecting me, I began to laugh. At that moment, I found such twisted humor in the depravity of my own soul. *I'm like a child throwing a tantrum to get my own way!* I tried to explain this to Patricia, who did the best she could to translate what I said into Portuguese for our host couple. Patricia started to join me in the giggles, and pretty soon everyone at our table was doubled over in laughter.

I learned through that experience that when God puts an immovable wall to block our path, he just might be trying to tell us something. We often attribute roadblocks to Satan, and sometimes it is the case. But perhaps when we try to overcome those road-blocks, we are in fact protesting God himself. Could God actually thwart our plans in order to protect us? *Maybe God really is keeping me waiting because he has something else, something better....*

Late that night, negative thought came at me again. *You're no good. You're just an amateur. That's why the record companies don't want you—not in Nashville, not in Tokyo, not anywhere.*

But this time I fought them. *Maybe,* I told myself, *God has blocked record companies from signing me because he wants to be the sole driver of my musical career.*

Could it be that he wanted my success attributed completely to him, not some carefully orchestrated plan by managers, agents, or labels? He is a jealous God, after all. He wants us to worship no other gods. A career in the high-pressured music industry might very well work out for some people, but for me... Well, maybe he knew

I would fall into a trap if I went that route. Maybe he was actually protecting me. *Thank you, Lord, for your infinite wisdom,* I prayed.

Then, and only then, was I able to sleep peacefully until dawn.

THE NEXT DAY WE AWOKE AT 4 A.M. TO head to the airport. We wanted to be there as early as possible to get a jump on the waiting list. We still hadn't completely given up.

It was a rainy morning. Thunder roared and lightning flashed in the predawn sky. We arrived at the regional airport by 5:00, and the place was already bustling with fellow holiday travelers, all jockeying for position on that all-important flight.

The humidity was high, and tempers were flaring. The ticket counter was about five people deep with travelers shouting at airline workers, who were already starting to sweat. I was still at number twenty-three on the waiting list. We just had to wait and see if I could eventually get on that flight.

At around 7:00, there was an announcement over the loudspeaker. Everyone quieted down to listen. I couldn't understand the Portuguese, but I could tell it was not good news. The entire airport let out a collective groan as Patricia translated: "The 9 a.m. inbound flight has been diverted to another city due to mechanical problems, and it is now delayed indefinitely. Possibly six or eight hours."

GROAN! I could picture David's disappointed face. Desperation set in. (Apparently, whatever lesson I learned the night before about God's protection flew right out of my brain as I got caught up in the moment.) I stomped my way over to the airline service desk, slapped my passport on the counter, and began speaking English to the ticketing agent in a not-so-Christian manner.

Suddenly, Patricia called out to me, "Wait, Junko! Wait!"

When I turned toward her, I noticed something: the airport had cleared out. It was now almost empty! Evidently, the announcement made everyone decide to abandon their holiday plans and, rather than wait hours for a delayed flight, head home.

The rain had stopped and the sun now peeked out from between the clouds. The air felt almost tropical—I could feel a warm breeze on my back. Patricia said, "There is no more waiting list. You are on my flight, if and when it actually gets here!"

Whew! Now I might possibly catch that flight back to Sao Paulo and go home. Overjoyed, I reached to hug her—when suddenly we heard another announcement.

Patricia let out a shriek of delight. "The previous announcement about the mechanical trouble on the inbound flight is canceled. The plane wasn't diverted after all; it's landing in thirty minutes!"

I could not believe my ears. This turn of events was so unexpected, so…God! *Thank you, Lord. Thank you for looking out for us.*

An hour later, as our plane to Sao Paulo made its ascent, I sat back in my seat and reflected on the events of that day and the previous night. We had just witnessed a miracle. God parted the Red Sea right there at the Belem Regional Airport, and Patricia and I marched over dry ground, through security, to our gate.

And to think what I would have missed out on had I gotten my way. I pictured God doubling over in laughter. Then the thought crossed my mind that the last few rumblings of the passing storm that morning weren't the angry rolls of thunder; they were his deep and resounding belly laughs. I was hearing Mr. Thunder's laughter!

God, you take such good care of me. You are never out to punish me or rob me of my joy. How did I ever think of you as the always angry Mr. Thunder? All along, you wanted the best for me.

I remembered the kind stranger's words. "Sometimes God keeps you waiting because he has something better in mind for you."

Thank you, Lord, for keeping me waiting.

I CAUGHT MY FLIGHT BACK TO LOS ANGELES in plenty of time and reunited with David. I shared all that happened in Brazil, particularly at my last stop in Belem. He was in tears when I got to the part about God's miracle at the airport. Although David hadn't been able to travel with me, he saw the power of God at work in my life.

After I got settled back home, I called the JEMS office to see how much total support money had come in. Before I left, I had raised enough support (though not 100 percent) for clearance to depart on my trip, but I had never gotten the final word. The secretary, Liliane, put me on hold so she could go find my files. When she came back on the line, she told me, "Three thousand, six hundred and fifty-five dolars."

I laughed. "No, Liliane, that's the total amount I was supposed to raise. I'm asking how much support money came in."

Liliane sounded puzzled. "It says here '$3655.' Let me check with the treasurer. May I put you on hold?" When she came back a minute later, she too was laughing. "Junko, that *is* the amount of money raised. The exact amount you needed. Praise the Lord!"

I was floored. The support letter that I had been so reluctant to write—the step I nearly didn't take because it felt humiliating—was blessed by God. Now, yet another miracle.

If I hadn't been obedient and written that support letter—if I had figured out a way to circumvent the whole support-raising process—then I would have totally missed out on seeing the miracle of a perfect match between my support need and the amount God provided. Wow, another near miss!

In the interest of full disclosure, I must tell you that over the following weeks a few more checks trickled in. I ended up with a surplus of several hundred dollars, which was disbursed to other ministry needs. Still, the point is that at the very moment I needed assurance of God's provision, he showed me again that he is faithful.

You know what I find amazing? If any of my supporters to that point had varied their support level by even one dollar—including folks who were able to support me in prayer alone—the math would have been off. I would not have witnessed this miracle of God's perfect provision.

Next time you receive a letter asking you to support missions work, know that you are taking part in a miracle. Prayerfully ask God what amount, if any, you ought to give. He is going to do great things!

SOON AFTER MY THREE WEEKS IN BRAZIL, I received a phone call from Ramona from *Today's Christian Woman* magazine. She wanted to let me know that not only did the editorial board approve my interview; they wanted to make it their cover story for the March/April 1996 issue.

I am going to be on the cover of a magazine? I couldn't wait to read "Junko Cheng's Secret to Contentment"—Ramona's account of my journey from Japan to the U.S. where, by God's grace, I ultimately found peace and contentment in him, my good and gracious God.

I was thrilled beyond words that God would use my story to

display his glory. *I hope people will take something away from it. And…I hope at least one person reads it!*

*I*N APRIL OF 1996, I AGAIN ATTENDED GMA in Nashville. As I grabbed all the usual freebies—pens, mugs, T-shirts, and magazines—I came across the *Christianity Today* booth. They had stacks of magazines to give away, including *Today's Christian Woman*. When I approached the stack, I saw something very familiar on the cover—a picture of me! Here at GMA they were giving away the very issue that featured my story!

I excitedly scooped up a handful of magazines (while both apologizing to and thanking the staff at the booth) and ran outside to call my husband. "Unbelievable!" was his reply. By this time, though, we had seen God do so many miracles that we were asking ourselves, "What's next?"

Who could have planned this turn of events? Only God, with his infinite wisdom…and his celestial sense of humor.

For the rest of the week, I walked around GMA in amazement. My face was everywhere! John Mays and Tom Jackson had never seen anything like it before. They were both so happy for me.

I was reminded of God's words to me through that Brazilian man: *Junko, I kept you waiting because I had something better for you.*

By this GMA, Jars of Clay was a phenomenon that no one in the Christian music industry could have ever imagined. Most of the A&R people from 1993 had either completely forgotten about me or no longer held the same position at their company. The CCM style had continued to evolve, and now my music captured even less of that industry's attention.

For many artists, CCM is a perfect fit and both parties benefit from the relationship. Clearly, that is God's plan for those artists. But he had a different plan carefully laid out for me. I could clearly see my music ministry moving in a different trajectory from the Nashville music industry.

That was the last year I attended GMA week.

GOD SHOWED ME THROUGH MY EXPERIENCE in Brazil that he is powerful, real, gracious, kind, and most of all good. Not long after my trip, he turned my attention to this passage from Psalms:

> LORD, *you have assigned me my portion and my cup;*
> *you have made my lot secure.*
> *The boundary lines have fallen for me in pleasant places;*
> *surely I have a delightful inheritance.*
> (Psalm 16:5–6)

What a blessing to know that God has specifically assigned my portion and made my lot secure. That lot may not be the same as that of Jars of Clay or several other friends who actually did sign record deals and go on to be blessed with brilliant careers in the Christian music industry.

But God is certainly looking out for me.

13

GOD'S WAYS
ARE NOT MY WAYS

Better a poor but wise youth than an old but
foolish king who no longer knows how to take warning.
ECCLESIASTES 4:13

S oon after I returned home from Nashville's GMA Spotlight
'93 competition, my pastor at the time, Mark Roberts,
invited me into his office for a chat. After congratulating
me on my win, he turned very serious.

"While I am excited about your music ministry expanding, I
don't want you to lose yourself in it, Junko," he said. "During the
years I spent on staff at Hollywood Presbyterian Church, I saw far
too many Christians who experienced great success in their career
but lost themselves along the way. They began to believe their own
press, and they slowly walked away from the church and, ultimately,
from God. In time, many of them lost their families, their marriages,
themselves. You are on your way to a career that might explode.
You might be on the verge of great success in the Christian music

industry. I don't want you to lose your footing and become one of those who lost themselves."

As you know by now, my career never really exploded. Instead, it continued on a slow, smooth trajectory to where it is now. But I appreciated my pastor for taking the time to talk with me about the pitfalls of fame and fortune. He spoke words that may have been hard for me to hear, in order to help me—his congregant and friend—not stumble in my Christian walk.

Before I learned some of the harsh realities of the music business, I had no idea what can happen to an artist whose song hits number one on the charts. Your life can be turned upside down overnight! Within days of a song hitting the radio airwaves, you might be packing your bags to go on the road for weeks, if not months. You literally walk away from daily life to travel constantly. You live on a tour bus, surrounded by people whose jobs depend on your success.

All of this can start to warp your sense of reality. Along with greater success comes isolation: you have contact with people whose sole job is to serve you. When the PR department circulates press releases filled with superlatives, you will find it more and more difficult to remember that you are a mere mortal—a sinner in need of a Savior, just like every other human being.

And all this happens in the *Christian* music business!

Pastor Mark has known people who didn't survive this type of a life. He knew how difficult it is to stay grounded once the bus starts rolling. I greatly appreciated that he waved that red flag before I got too far along in my music career. An up-front warning is far better than trying to perform damage control afterward!

Besides, I never want to be onstage singing about a God I used to know. I always want my testimony to ring genuine and true, for my convictions to remain honest and real. Had I become an overnight sensation, I would have been more aware of the potential pitfalls because my pastor demonstrated courage and compassion in talking to me that day. Though Pastor Mark has since moved on to a different ministry in Texas, David and I still consider him one of our dearest friends and our pastor.

When I embarked on my music career, God called me in for a face-to-face just as Pastor Mark had. And I could not deny his message to me: "I am the LORD your God."

Until I began my own music ministry, I didn't fully understand that this great God is in control of everything. Sure, I had the fundamentals down; I could cite verses to back up the basic tenets of my Christian faith. But I didn't know—truly know, in an intimate way—the living God who is above all…yet loves me deeply.

When I began my itinerant music ministry, I became aware that people listen to what I say simply because I sing. I was given a pulpit, and with it came great responsibility.

This realization spurred me to get more serious about studying the Bible and nailing down basic theology. People listen intently to my testimony and whatever banter I offer between my songs, and I never want to mislead anyone.

(This is one reason I am concerned when young, new Christian artists with great voices—but not much in the way of life experience or godly wisdom—are immediately sent out on the concert circuit. I hope and pray these young musicians receive solid biblical guidance and counsel. Otherwise, it won't be long before they make statements that are at best regretful, and at worst blasphemous.)

In the process of learning more about my God, the Almighty, I developed a truly passionate relationship with the Lord. Sometimes I tell people that possibly the biggest beneficiary of my own ministry has been me!

I cannot imagine how ineffective I would have been had I embarked on my ministry with the idea that God is the angry Mr. Thunder I once believed in. If I were in an audience and heard a message like that, I would run from such a God!

Or how about that perfectionistic God who was so demanding that I almost gave up trying to please him? I might have convicted a lot of people of sin, but I wouldn't have clearly guided them toward forgiveness and grace. And that omission wouldn't have been intentional—at the time, I didn't really understand sin or forgiveness either. Praise God that nothing is wasted in his economy, and that he can and does use my past misunderstandings and burdens for his glory!

These days, I meet a lot of people who are confused about Christianity and feel burdened by "this whole religion thing." I am able to sit down with them and, by sharing from my own life experiences, help them move toward an accurate and saving knowledge of God.

I was so fearful of God at the beginning of my life. Now, I am so in love with him. I know he cares about me and loves me so much that he was willing to die for me.

And he prays for me! I was thrilled to read this one day:

My prayer is not for them alone. I pray also for those who will believe in me through their message, that all of them may be one, Father, just as you are in me and I am in you. May they also be in us so that the world may believe that you have sent me. (John 17:20)

Before he went to the cross, Jesus personally prayed for all future believers, and that includes me. Yes, he was down on his knees talking to his Father, and he prayed for me. And he prayed for you, too!

$\mathscr{R}$ECENTLY, DESPITE AN INJURY ON HER right foot, my ten-year-old daughter, Megumi, worked hard to prepare for an audition at her dance studio. My twelve-year-old son did his own hard work—waiting patiently at the dance studio during the audition. For about two hours, Josh sat amongst a sea of aspiring dancers (almost all girls) doing his homework. I felt that they both deserved a little reward, so afterward I took them to a market near the dance studio to buy them each a mechanical pencil that they had been wanting. It's a nifty little invention. You shake it, and the lead comes out. No more clicking at the top end! It wasn't expensive, and it made them both very happy.

I used to think that life was like what my kids experienced that afternoon: you work hard for something or endure hardship for a season, and eventually you will be rewarded. The reward might be the very thing you were working for. At the very least, you would enjoy a sense of accomplishment and the will to pursue another goal.

In any case, we expect a reward for good work and persever-ance—and we want it now! We certainly aren't satisfied with the notion that our reward awaits us in heaven, true as it may be.

But life doesn't always work out the way we plan. Sometimes we don't get what we want no matter how hard we try or how diligently we work. I could cry foul, shake my fist at God for being so unfair, and throw a tantrum that would outdo any two-year-old.

Fortunately, I've since learned how damaging that way of think-ing can be. In fact, several instances of my *not* getting what I strongly desire—to fit in with my peers, gain worldly fame and success in my music career, or have a guaranteed seat on an important flight—have led to much bigger payoffs.

Through those experiences I learned that God is so much bigger than I ever imagined. As a result, I enjoyed deeper intimacy in my relationship with him.

Had I gotten my way every time, I might never have understood the true power of this great and wonderful God. Instead, I would have felt pretty proud of my own accomplishments and not much need for a loving Savior.

I'll share with you one huge reward I received from God, though—something I desired for a long, long time and which God was gracious enough to grant me during my lifetime.

Recently, a congregational meeting at our church was preceded by—you guessed it—an ice cream social. As I worked my way down the line with David and our children, it dawned on me that this was exactly what I had desperately wished for more than thirty years earlier. Here I was, with my own family, attending an ice cream social!

Holding the sticky ice cream scoop in my hand, I excitedly told everyone in line, "Back when I was in sixth grade I *so* wanted to attend an ice cream social with my own family. And look— here I am!"

The people around me smiled and nodded, but no one really appreciated the magnitude of this momentous occasion, not even my kids ("That's nice, mom"). Who could blame them?

As I poured syrup over my ice cream creation, I repeated to no one in particular, "It's true! I'm at an ice cream social with my husband and kids…. Thank you, Lord."

Only David gave me a knowing smile, and that was more than enough for me.

MANY OF US SHORT-CIRCUIT GOD'S work in our lives and miss out on seeing his magnificent power as he orchestrates the days, months, years of our life. When we find ourselves in difficult situations, we either manipulate the circumstances to get what we want, or we give up and walk away. "It just didn't work for me," we might shrug.

But really, who are we to know what is best for us? Who are we to question what God decides to do?

Look at these verses:

What then shall we say? Is God unjust? Not at all! For he says to Moses, "I will have mercy on whom I have mercy, and I will have compassion on whom I have compassion."

It does not, therefore, depend on man's desire or effort, but on God's mercy. For the Scripture says to Pharaoh: "I raised you up for this very purpose, that I might display my power in you and that my name might be proclaimed in all the earth." Therefore God has mercy on whom he wants to have mercy, and he hardens whom he wants to harden. (Romans 9:14–18)

During my travels in Brazil, I learned in a new way that God is all-powerful. He can give us something or take it away—it's completely up to him. Sometimes life events don't make sense at all, but he does what he does and allows what he allows because he is much wiser than any of us.

He doesn't do things on a whim, as we humans sometimes do. Nor does he do anything with evil intent. God is a benevolent God: he always watches out for us. Sometimes God keeps us waiting because he has something better in mind for us. Something much, much better!

When I realized how powerful God is, I was struck by reverent fear. This wasn't the same kind of fear I experienced as a little girl in Japan, cowering behind the furniture during thunderstorms. Back then, I was deathly afraid of a very angry Mr. Thunder.

It took many years, but God slowly revealed his gentle side to me so that I would know beyond a shadow of a doubt that he is good. Evidently he thought that I had progressed to the point of being ready to see him reveal his full glory. He certainly did that during my trip to Brazil.

I have come full circle. Once again I fear God, but this is a reverent fear that only our heavenly Father, the one true God, the Creator of heaven and earth, deserves. This kind of fear is the beginning of wisdom (Proverbs 1:7).

It is my prayer that you will come to know, to love, and to stand in awe before God—my Mr. Thunder—as I have.

ABOUT THE AUTHOR

*J*unko (June-Co) Nishiguchi Cheng is an award-winning Japanese American singer/songwriter who began her singing career on NHK television in Tokyo. She continues to record and travel internationally with her ministry, with an emphasis on singing for children. She has opened for artists such as Michael W. Smith and Avalon, and for speakers such as John Townsend and Tony Campolo. Junko has been featured on *Focus on the Family* radio, in *Worship Leader* magazine, and was a cover interview for *Today's Christian Woman* magazine. She makes her home with her husband, David, and their two children in Irvine, California, where she is also a worship leader at Saddleback Church. Find out more about Junko at www.junko.com.

CPSIA information can be obtained at www.ICGtesting.com
Printed in the USA
BVOW08s1815131015

422278BV00001B/16/P